The

SCIENCE

OF

DEER
HUNTING

by John E. Phillips

Book 2 in the Deer Hunting Library
by Larsen's Outdoor Publishing

Copyright (c) 1992 by John E. Phillips

All rights reserved. No part of this book may be reproduced or transmitted in any form of by any means, electronic or mechanical, including photocopying, recording, or by any information storage and retrieval system, without permission in writing from the publisher.

ISBN 0-936513-22-5

Library of Congress 92-071317

Published by:

LARSEN'S OUTDOOR PUBLISHING
2640 Elizabeth Place
Lakeland, FL 33813

PRINTED IN THE UNITED STATES OF AMERICA

5 6 7 8 9 10

DEDICATION

She has stumbled and fallen in beaver swamps, crawled through briar patches, climbed mountains and stayed up all day and night to be able to hunt. She has proven she is an outdoor journalist and a good friend. This book is dedicated to Laurie Lee Dovey. Thanks, pal!

ACKNOWLEDGMENTS

Many hands, minds and hearts must work together to make up the spirit and content of a book. In this volume, the knowledge that many great deer hunters and wildlife researchers have shared enable me to transfer it to you.

Also numbers of people have labored long and hard to bring this volume to you including my wife, Denise Phillips, Marjolyn McLellan, Margaret Smith, Elizabeth Tittle, Kirsten Hunt, Carol Evans, Mary Ann Armstrong and Cara Clark. The cover artist, John P. Lee, has produced a striking portrayal of fighting bucks.

Too a bond of faith, trust, respect and confidence must be developed between an author and the publisher for any book to reach print. All these elements have been present with my publishers and friends, Larry and Lilliam Larsen, who have worked diligently and patiently to see this book through to the end.

I am only the author who labors in the field of words with these co-workers.

PREFACE

When I was a teenager, I often slept in the woods. I would snuggle deep in my rainsuit and was lulled to sleep frequently by the gentle sound of rain tapping on my suit.

One night, I was awakened at 3:00 A.M. by a dog in the distance baying at fleeing deer. I did not want to totally wake up. Slightly cracking my right eye open, I saw the vision of an eight point buck standing not 30 yards away from me. Closing my eyes once more, I questioned the vision I had seen.

This time both of my eyes came open together. The buck actually was standing and feeding not 30 yards from me. I brought my daddy's old shotgun to my shoulder and rested the bead on the end of the barrel right behind the deer's front shoulder. As gently as I would hold an egg, I slid the safety to the fire position and squeezed the trigger. When the buck went down, I sealed forever my fate as a deer hunter and began my never-ending quest for more knowledge about deer hunting.

The sport of deer hunting is one you continue to learn throughout your life. This book, THE SCIENCE OF DEER HUNTING, contains the most recent information on deer from the best experts throughout the nation.

CONTENTS

Acknowledgements 5
Preface 9
About The Author 11

1   How To Hunt Deer Scientifically 13
2   How To Think Like A Buck 19
3   How To Set Up A Half-Mile Deer Hunt 29
4   How To Know When Deer Move 37
5   How Moonlight Affects Buck Behavior 45
6   How Much Pressure Can A Buck Stand 53
7   How Effective Are Scents 61
8   Why Bucks Fight 71
9   The Weatherman Can Help You Hunt Better 81
10 Why Nuts Are The Best Bet For Bucks 89
11 Hunting Deer On Trails 97
12 The Truth About The Rut 109
13 Hunting The Rut 119
14 Facts & Myths About Antlers 127
15 Truth And Fiction About Deer Tracks 135
16 Tracking And Trailing Deer 143
Index 151
Fishing & Hunting Resource Directory 155

ABOUT THE AUTHOR

For more than three decades, John E. Phillips has hunted whitetail deer. He even chose to attend Livingston University in deer-rich Southwest Alabama to be able to deer hunt daily during Alabama's liberal deer season, which runs 3-1/2-months each year, during his college years until graduation.

Phillips also has been a student of deer and deer hunting as an active outdoor writer and photographer for more than 20-years for both newspapers and magazines. Phillips, the author of 11 outdoor books including: *The Masters' Secrets of Turkey Hunting, The Masters' Secrets of Deer Hunting, Doubleday's Turkey Hunter's Bible, Alabama Outdoors Cookbook, How To Make More Profits In Taxidermy, Catch More Crappie, Outdoor Life's Complete Turkey Hunting, Bass Fishing With The Skeeter Pros, North American Hunting Club's Turkey Hunting Tactics, Deer & Fixings* and *Fish and Fixings,* has had more than 1100 articles published on deer hunting.

An active member of the Outdoor Writers Association of America, the Southeastern Outdoors Press Association, the Alabama Press Association, the Alabama Sportswriters' Association and Outdoors Photographic League, Phillips has won numerous awards for excellence in writing magazine and newspaper articles and outdoor books.

Phillips feels fortunate to have hunted with some of the greatest deer hunters of our day, to have interviewed and learned from the leading scientific researchers in the field of deer behavior and to have hunted deer across the U.S.

CHAPTER 1

HOW TO HUNT DEER SCIENTIFICALLY

IS THERE A BETTER WAY, a more scientific way to hunt deer? Can we use scientific information to plan our hunting strategies?

The answer to these questions is yes. But hunting cannot be best learned by reading textbooks. Since conditions change throughout the day, knowing when to leave a tactic and/or change strategies is as critical to successful hunting as the wealth of information the hunter takes into the woods with him.

To discover how to hunt more scientifically, I talked with Dr. Billy Hillestad of Kennesaw, Georgia, who has a PhD in wildlife ecology, a master's degree in wildlife management and has taken more than 200 deer in his lifetime. Hillestad has studied population dynamics and the behavior of deer throughout his academic career. As a hunter, Dr. Hillestad has spent thousands of hours not only learning how and where to take deer more effectively but also understanding the basic nature of the deer by attempting to pre-determine when, where and why a buck will show up at certain places in the woods.

Hillestad's goal is to spend most of the time he has to hunt in the most productive area of the woods trying to take a whitetail. To hunt more efficiently, Hillestad draws on his education and knowledge of deer to help him determine where and when a buck may appear and how to best approach the animal without spooking

To take a buck like this, you must learn to hunt scientifically.

him. When Hillestad hunts a new area he's never been in before, his goal is to read the signs, find a buck and attempt to bag him.

Tactic: Read The Terrain As You Enter The Region

"On the way to the spot where I plan to begin my hunt, I notice the terrain," Dr. Hillestad explains. "For instance, if I see a small stream I know a creek bottom will be running through my stalk area, which should provide some hardwood timber and good habitat for deer. Also I assume mast trees and acorn trees will be somewhere in that stream bottom. Although this data may seem insignificant, I take note and file the information away for future reference.

"I also observe as I enter my hunt area if any supplemental food plots like greenfields are present and which roads or paths in the area pass by the greenfields."

Tactic: Know The Weather Forecast
Before You Hunt

"If a cold front is moving in, a deer will be filling its belly with food before it comes into an area," Dr. Hillestad reports. "When a cold front arrives, deer in the affected region lose much heat and many calories. A deer requires more food than usual to sustain itself in colder weather and will eat more heavily just before a front."

Tactic: Read The Signs Deer Leave In Your Area
And Link The Evidence Together

Hillestad emphasizes beginning to hunt where you see tracks and signs. "Remember oftentimes the best place to hunt may be right where you start to hunt -- rather than a half-mile further in the woods. Don't overlook obvious deer sign just because you're only 10 to 20 yards from your vehicle.

"If you see the tracks and sign showing deer have fed on a food plot, then realize the next place they probably will go is to a bedding area in the early morning. If possible use a path or an old logging road, which will enable you to move quickly and quietly, to pass the greenfield and look for the closest thick cover where the deer can bed. Because deer prefer diversity of habitat, clearcut areas provide an ideal place for deer to bed in the early morning. Usually if deer have fed all night, they will be lying in heavy cover at daybreak."

Tactic: Take Into Consideration When The Rut
Occurs Where You Are Hunting

"The only reason bucks won't be bedding in the early morning is if a doe is in estrus," Dr. Hillestad mentions. "Then you may spot a buck following a doe. However, if you are hunting during the pre-rut, the likelihood of catching a buck up and moving during the early morning hours is remote."

Tactic: Learn To Read How Fresh Buck Sign Is

According to Hillestad, if you locate a rub on a tree where a young buck has rubbed his antlers, "You can determine if the rub is fresh, because the bark on the tree will be freshly peeled and not have changed color very much. Bark becomes more discolored the more time that has elapsed since it has been rubbed.

"Deer most often like to rub trees that are aromatic like cedar and pine and will leave a scent when they're scraped. By taking your pocket knife and scraping the kinds of trees you see deer rubbing and observing the trees you've scraped in an hour, two hours, four hours, six hours and eight hours, you soon can learn to recognize how old a rub is. Knowing how much time has passed from the time the deer has rubbed the tree until you observe the rub can be critical in determining how close you are to the buck you want to take.

"Another way to pinpoint the time a rub has been made is to notice whether the shavings from that rub are in a nice, neat, little pile at the base of a tree, which means the shavings have not been blown by the wind or disturbed by other animals. If the tree is small in diameter, the rub probably has been made by a small buck. Through the years, I have learned that small bucks use little trees to rub. I've never seen a big buck rubbing a small tree.

"But no piece of evidence is enough to form the foundation of any conclusion. You need supporting evidence to document any theory. So with my 'small bucks rub small trees' theory I have substantiated this idea with the fact that when I see small trees rubbed, the rubs are always closer to the ground, indicating the deer itself is smaller and closer to the ground. If you're lucky enough to see a deer in the woods rubbing a tree, or if you watch deer in a pen, the bigger, taller, more robust bucks scrape trees higher than little bucks do.

"Also remember a buck pushes hard to scrape the bark off those trees, and the larger trees offer more resistance to the bigger bucks. The main range of the heavy scraping for a young buck will be about a foot above the ground. The main range of rubs made by a larger buck will be about two feet off the ground. There may be marks above and below the main area of scraping, but generally I believe the hunter can say that big bucks scrape big trees and their rubs will be higher off the ground than the rubs of little bucks. Bucks usually begin a great deal of rubbing activity just prior to the rut and just before initiating scrapes."

Tactic: Be Conscious Of The Wind Direction

"I have found when the wind is continuously variable, hunters are at a real disadvantage -- if they are stalk hunting," Hillestad comments. "To hunt deer successfully, you must have a favorable wind. Many a hunt is spoiled when the hunter is stalking a deer, and

Binoculars can be an asset to the hunter and enable him to see deer at greater distances.

the wind direction alters -- carrying his scent to the deer before the hunter has the opportunity to see and take the animal. When wind becomes variable, I discontinue my hunt and wait for a steady wind direction.

"Then when the wind steadies, I'll resume my hunt for buck sign. Searching for sign to lead you to a buck is a much more effective way of hunting than merely walking through the woods looking for deer.

17

My technique of hunting is to discover the sign, be able to read the sign and then realize the sign will lead me to my buck."

Tactic: Use Binoculars To See Deer At Greater Distances And Hunt Cover Closer

"I always use my binoculars to look into thick cover which deer love, long before I approach it, which is another key to successful hunting that will pay buck dividends," Dr. Hillestad emphasizes. "When you see cover, hunt that cover assuming the deer is there.

"Binoculars also can save you much walking. Often with binoculars I can tell if a rub is fresh or not fresh and can visually cover much more ground with my eyes than I can with my feet."

Tactic: Eliminate Hunting Areas Where You Don't Think A Buck Will Be

As Dr. Hillestad says, "I often don't hunt through a creek bottom because the area is wide open. Although you may spot a little buck moving through an open place like this, I have found that most often the bigger trophy bucks will be holding in thick cover. Therefore I eliminate the portions of the woods that don't provide the type of cover where deer prefer to bed and concentrate my hunting time in the regions where deer should be. If you can locate a section with various kinds of habitat like young pines with a few sweet gums growing near them and a transition of habitat, this area will be where deer prefer to travel.

"To me, the most exciting hunt for a true trophy whitetail is when you know a trophy is in front of you, and the deer realizes you're out there somewhere. Both of you must rely on your skill, instincts and judgment to elude each other."

From interviewing Dr. Hillestad, I have learned that successful, scientific deer hunting is much like trying to solve a mystery. A good investigator never looks for the criminal but instead searches diligently for the clues and studies the evidence that will lead him to the place to catch his adversary.

CHAPTER 2

HOW TO THINK LIKE A BUCK

Patterning has become a term used quite frequently in the out-of-doors. Fishermen talk about patterning bass, duck hunters speak of patterning waterfowl, and deer hunters discuss patterning deer. What few of us fail to realize is that deer pattern people to survive. The older the buck, the quicker he learns to pattern hunters.

The greater the hunting pressure, the easier the people and the deer are to pattern. Young bucks often die quick. Older bucks that rely on their instincts from years past know when, where and how to retreat for cover when man enters the woods. If you are going to take a woods wizard, you must understand the mature buck deer and be able to think like he does. Each buck in every situation is different, but let's look at some examples of how to hunt the monarch of the woods.

The Field Buck

The field buck is a wise, older deer that can be seen feeding in fields and pastures all summer long and at the beginning of hunting season. But just about the time the sportsman decides to enter the woods, the buck vanishes. He can be spotted in the field at night, but rarely will he be seen during daylight hours. This buck realizes danger is in the woods when hunting season begins.

Since we know the buck is feeding in the field at night, the trick to bagging him is to find the route he takes to and from the field. After dark, navigation through the woods can be the key to taking that buck of a lifetime. You will find the later in the season you try to hunt a field buck, the further he will be away from the field during daylight hours. But by following this buck's travel lane from his field to his bedding area, you have two chances of bagging him -- at first light or 30 minutes before dark.

Once you have established the buck's route from the field to the bedding area and have picked out a tree to put your stand in, go to that stand well before daylight. This will require navigation skills using a compass and possibly marking a trail. To learn how to utilize a compass, order the Brunton Company's detailed and informative video, "The ABC's of Maps and Compasses," from 620 East Monroe, Riverton, WY 82501, Phone: 307-856-6559.

When you know how to use a compass, arrive at the tree 45 minutes to an hour before sunrise. You only may have 15 to 20 minutes of hunting time at first light when the buck leaves the field and heads for his bedding site.

The other chance you have at this buck will come 30 minutes before dark. In studying bucks on hunting preserves where greenfield hunting is the only means utilized for harvest, many sportsmen have learned that trophy deer have what is called a staging area -- a region the deer come to and wait for nightfall before entering a field. This staging area usually will be from 100 to 300 yards away from the field. If you can be in a tree 1-1/2-hours before dark and stay until dark, you may get a shot at that trophy buck when he arrives at his staging area. Remember, the deer knows when and where hunters will appear, because he has patterned hunters. To take one of these old, wise bucks, you must be in an area at a time when usually a hunter never shows up.

Honey Hole Deer

Since the older, bigger, smarter bucks learn quickly to pattern hunters and how to avoid them, during hunting season in high hunter pressure regions, these bucks will stay in what I call honey holes. A honey hole is a place where the buck will be safe from the hunter and where the hunter rarely thinks of looking for a buck.

Some honey holes I have encountered have been ditches right beside main roads leading to hunting camps. The buck soon learns that vehicles go up and down the road during hunting season, but no one ever stops to hunt these places -- assuming that the traffic up and down the road spooks the deer. However, mature deer have learned the vehicles themselves pose no threat -- what's in the

In thick cover areas, bow hunters may have an advantage over gun hunters.

vehicle brings the harm. So these ditches along the sides of main roads provide sanctuary for trophy bucks.

Another honey hole I found one time was a briar patch within 50 yards of a busy camphouse. A big, smart buck had learned he could lie in that briar thicket during daylight hours, slip in and out of the thicket after dark and stay safe from hunters all season long. A biologist from Mississippi once told me that when he flew over cotton fields in heavily hunted areas, he often spotted trophy bucks lying in the middle of the cotton fields. Although the hunters were in the woods, the big deer were hidden in the cotton fields where the sportsmen never thought to look.

Other outdoorsmen have taken trophy bucks along an escape route within 100 yards of where hunters park their vehicles to go into the woods. Some older, wiser bucks will bed close to the road and flee into the woods when the first car doors slam, using the escape route to go deep into the woods before the hunters ever enter the forest.

To find one of these honey holes that may contain a trophy buck, obtain an aerial photograph of the land you hunt. Use magic markers to draw a flow chart showing where most of the sportsmen enter the woods and where they hunt. As you diagram the hunting pressure, you soon will be able to learn where the bucks must be to survive. If you will hunt the places no one else does, you will bag a honey hole buck.

Maps To Help You Hunt Bucks

Various maps are available to help sportsmen hunt more effectively as well as have an inexpensive, nearby place to camp. Here's a list of some of the places you can write to learn that information.

(1) U. S. Geological Survey, Federal Center, Building 41,
    P. O. Box 25286, Denver, Colorado 80225

Purchase indexes and order forms for the maps of states West of the Mississippi River, including Alaska and Hawaii, from this address. The U. S. Geological Survey, which has mapped the entire United States, has topographical maps to scale available at $2.50 each that contain line and symbol representations of natural terrain and manmade structures. These maps will aid a hunter in determining where roads, rivers, firebreaks and property lines are on a specific piece of property. Most outdoorsmen prefer the 22" x 27" maps, which depict on a large scale the amount of land a hunter usually can walk in a day.

The indexes of the topographical maps name the region covered by each map, the scale available and the year the area was surveyed. These indexes also include lists of special maps that have been made of a place as well as the names and addresses of map dealers, map reference libraries and federal distribution centers.

"Topographical Map Symbols," "Topographical Maps: Silent Guides for the Outdoorsman" and "Maps for America: Cartographic Products of the U.S. Geological Survey and Others" are pamphlets available from either of the U. S. Geological Survey centers that help explain the various kinds of maps as well as the meanings of the symbols, lines, etc. on them maps.

(2) U. S. Geological Survey, 1200 South Eads Street
    Arlington, VA 22202

Use this address to order topographical maps for states East of the Mississippi River.

(3) Local libraries - Many local libraries have sets of topographical maps available as well as order forms and indexes for the maps. Also the library near the place where you plan to hunt may contain maps of that county that are not accessible in other parts of the state.

(4) Division of Wildlife Refuges, c/o U. S. Fish and Wildlife
    Service, Department of the Interior, Room 2343
    Washington, D. C. 20402

This department distributes free maps, which will help hunters determine the best places to set up on nearby lands, of the more than 400 wildlife refuges under federal protection.

(5) National Wetlands Inventory Office, c/o U. S. Fish and
    Wildlife Service, Department of the Interior
    Washington, D. C. 20204

Approximatcly 10,000 acres of wetlands are mapped by this group.

(6) Water and Power Resources Service, Office of Public Affairs
    Department of the Interior
    Washington, D. C. 20240

Write for free recreation maps of the facilities of this group, formerly the Bureau of Reclamation, across the United States at 333 reservoirs, including camping areas, etc.

(7) "Field Offices of the Forest Service" Pamphlet, Office of
    Public Affairs, Forest Service, Department of Agriculture
    South Building, Room 3008
    Washington, D. C. 20250

This free pamphlet lists the locations and addresses of all national forests and grasslands. Write the National Forest Service office nearest you to order maps of any of the 122 national forests, and indicate what types of activities you are planning, since the Forest Service sometimes produces different maps for hikers, hunters, campers, etc. The maps generally cost $1 - $2 each.

(8) U. S. Government Printing Office, Superintendent of
    Documents, Washington, D. C. 20402

By writing the above address or visiting the GPO nearest you, you can find many helpful pamphlets and maps.

"National Parks of the U. S. - Guide and Map" is a map available that shows the locations of the national parks and includes a chart listing the services, facilities and activities in each park.

"Maps and Atlases - SB-102" and "Surveying and Mapping - SB-183" are two subject bibliographies available free from the GPO too.

(9) U. S. Army Corps of Engineers, Office of Public Affairs
    Department of the Army, 2 Massachusetts Avenue, N. W.
    Washington, D. C. 20314

The Corps of Engineers produces and distributes maps of the recreation areas it manages, but each map must be ordered from the district where the recreational area is located. By writing the above address, you can learn the Corps' districts and addresses.

(10) Office of Public Affairs, Federal Energy Regulatory
     Commission, 825 North Capital Street, N. E.
     Washington, D. C. 20426

This commission can give you information about various maps available on the hydroelectric projects licensed by the U. S. Department of Energy where there are public facilities for hunting, camping and other activities.

(11) National Cartographic Information Center, 507 National
     Center, 12201 Sunrise Valley Drive
     or 345 Middlefield Road, Menlo Park, CA 94025

This center is the part of the U. S. Geological Survey that is the main source for maps that are produced or distributed by federal agencies, as well as by commercial publishers. Some of the free publications include, "Types of Maps Published by Government Agencies," "Finding Your Way With Map and Compass," and "Popular Publications of the U.S. Geological Survey."

(12) Defense Mapping Agency, Office of Distribution Services
     Department of the Army, ATTENTION: DDCP
     Washington, D. C. 20315

Write this source for information on topographical maps of the U. S. as contained in the "Catalog of Maps, Charts and Related Products."

(13) Bureau of Land Management - Learn the addresses of the BLM offices nearest to the land you plan to hunt by visiting your library and studying the "United States Government Organization Manual." The BLM offers access to some fine outdoor recreation in the western states and has a series of 60 minute quadrangle maps at a cost of $4 each that show land contours, roads, streams, lakes and manmade structures along with color codings to indicate whether the owner of the land is federal, state, private, etc.

(14) Federal Depository Libraries, Consumer Information Center, Pueblo, CO 81009

By contacting this center, you can receive a list of the public, college and government libraries throughout the U.S. that receive copies of most federal government publications, including maps.

(15) Large landholding companies in areas you plan to hunt, including timber companies, steel corporations, mining concerns and power companies will have maps available to show where permit hunting can be done.

Gun Hunter, Friend Of The Bowhunter

Often if you'll hunt with a bow during gun/deer season, you can increase your odds of bagging a buck. When gun season occurs at the same time as bow season, gun hunters create a great deal of noise, leave a lot of scent in the woods and usually spend more time walking than they do hunting. Since these actions break up the deer's normal feeding and bedding patterns, oftentimes the whitetail will be very difficult to find during gun/deer season. Many of the young bucks die quickly, while the old bucks become invisible.

But if you are hunting with a bow, the gun hunter very well may put that trophy in your lap -- if you think like the trophy deer. To survive, that buck must hole up in thick cover during daylight hours when hunting pressure is extremely high and not move very much. The trophy whitetail generally will be the safest in the most dense cover he can discover. Wise bucks realize most hunters will not penetrate thick cover to find them.

A bowman also must learn to think like the average gun hunter, who will hunt in areas that will allow him to take a shot at the maximum range of his weapon. Many shotgun deer hunters use the

3 inch magnum, which may have an effective range of 40 to 50 yards. The rifle hunter tends to choose the larger calibers and high-powered scopes to stretch his effective range out to 200 or 300 yards. If you're hunting with a weapon that will take a deer at 200 or 300 yards, then there is no reason to hunt the regions where your visibility is only from 15 to 30 yards. The gun hunter generally prefers to hunt open woods where his visibility matches the effective range of his weapon.

To set up an effective hunt plan with your bow, eliminate parts of the woods where you can see at distances greater than 40 yards, because that is where the gun hunter will be and where the trophy buck expects to encounter hunters. On an aerial photograph, cross out the parts of the woods where you have visibility of 50 yards or more. Then begin to concentrate your hunting time in the areas where visibility will be 30 yards or less.

Some of the most productive bowhunting spots where you are most likely to see a buck may have zero visibility, which will weed out all the hunters except the sportsmen who determine how to hunt these regions. Dr. Bob Sheppard of Carrollton, Alabama, a dedicated outdoorsman and an instructor in various schools for hunting deer with bow, blackpowder guns and conventional weapons, has solved this problem.

"Many times I will penetrate thick cover and use a pair of pruning shears to cut shooting lanes in the foliage," Sheppard mentions. "I don't cut a path into the thick cover. I may get down on my hands and knees and crawl. But once I arrive in these thick places like a briar thicket or a clearcut, I cut three shooting lanes in spoke fashion from my stand. The shooting lanes, which only may be three to four feet wide, may not run but 30 yards. However, if a deer is moving through that cover, I often can get a shot at him."

Because the gunman is hunting the open areas, he forces the deer into very small pockets that often are well within bow range. Reaching these protected pockets and deciding how and where to set up a stand to take a shot can be difficult.

Don Taylor of Birmingham, Alabama, a veteran trophy buck hunter of more than four decades, explains that, "Even the thickest cover has some kind of natural break in the foliage -- a drainage ditch, a small creek or an open spot. But many hunters are not willing to go through the agony of penetrating that dense cover to attempt to locate small clearings where they can take a shot.

A trophy buck often will put a doe or a smaller buck in front of him to look for harm.

However, these places are where the big bucks will stay when hunting pressure is high."

When you are hunting trophy deer with a bow, consider the gun hunter an asset. If you have the ability to think like a deer, the gun hunter will force the buck to be in specific areas usually with little visibility.

To be successful at bagging one of the bigger, smarter bucks, you must concentrate and stay alert for a longer time, which includes no sleeping in the treestand or letting your mind wander. In dense cover hunting, you only may have a few seconds to draw and shoot before the buck vanishes when the shot does present itself.

"For this reason when I'm hunting thick cover, I don't sit on my treestand," Dr. Sheppard says. "I stand up for the 1-1/2-hours I'm trying to arrow a deer. I believe I can concentrate more on my hunting, see more deer, take more shots and be more successful by staying on my feet than if I'm sitting down and casual hunting."

To hunt the trophy buck in high pressure areas during gun/deer season, you must maintain a high level of intensity and alertness to be ready for the shot when it presents itself.

The Decoy Deer

Old bucks have another survival tactic they use. They permit young bucks and does to die first. A trophy buck will sacrifice other deer in the herd before he will place himself in harm's way, because he has learned the hunter usually is attempting to bag any deer. Often a mature buck will allow does and young bucks to walk ahead of him, even when he is traveling in thick cover. If you plan to take that trophy buck, you must have nerves of steel and let does and smaller bucks pass under your stand, although they are within easy range. These are the decoy deer that move ahead of the woods' monarchs. Remember, if a trophy buck is not in the area you are hunting, you may be able to come back later and bag one of the smaller bucks or does.

Don't be fooled by the decoy deer. Instead use these deer to decoy the buck. Let them pass in front of you to prove to the older buck no danger is around him. Then when he walks out, you can bag him. This tactic requires patience and willpower. To outsmart this intelligent animal, we must reason like him and use the information the trophy buck has learned to cause his downfall.

The Trophy Buck During The Rut

During the rut, the dominant buck has the responsibility of breeding all the does that come into estrus within his home range. For this reason, he constantly must stay on the move and sometimes expose himself to the hunter. However, the more mature bucks that have survived several rutting seasons often will make their scrapes (areas where the bucks often breed the does) in thick cover to elude hunters. Check sites of heavy cover for scrapes to hunt in the rut.

The older and bigger the buck you want to take, the more he knows about you. Many mature bucks that are trophies and survivors have PhD's in hunter eluding. To bag a prize like this, you must reason like a buck.

CHAPTER 3

HOW TO SET UP A HALF-MILE
DEER HUNT

"YOU MAY HAVE too much land to hunt," I told a friend of mine as I watched the color drain from his face, his chin flop, his mouth open like the Grand Canyon, and his eyes roll back in his head. I already knew what he was going to say.

"You've lost your mind, John. Nobody has too much land to hunt. Actually most people don't have enough land to hunt. I don't believe any place in the world has enough land to hunt deer the way a sportsman wants to hunt."

This riddle of deer hunting may not have a simple answer. How much land does a deer hunter need to hunt deer? In the West, he'll require much more land than the eastern hunter does, because often the deer are spread out, the land is more open, and the habitat is not as thick. But in the forests East of the Mississippi River and in many areas of the Midwest and the Northwest, an outdoorsman may not need more than a half a mile to hunt.

Bass fishermen have much the same problem. Most professional bass anglers I know don't fish a lake or sometimes even a part of a lake. Usually they intensively angle 200 to 500 yards of shoreline.

The successful deer hunter can be much more effective in the areas where the terrain permits -- if he learns how to set up and hunt a specific half-mile of woods. Let's look at a half-mile hunt much like a bass fisherman targets a region to fish.

Why Shrink The Amount Of Woods & Waters

A lake with 500 miles of shoreline is too big to fish, just as a woodlot with 30,000 acres is too large a region to hunt. To decrease the size of the area he has to fish, the bass angler will determine where the bass will be because of their normal seasonal and migratory patterns. In the spring of the year, he knows the bass will be moving from deep water to shallow water to spawn. During the summer, he understands the fish are going from shallow water, which is hotter, to the deeper water, which is cooler. In the fall of the year, the bass will be leaving the deep water to travel into the shallow again. Then in the winter, the bass will be moving into the deeper holes, while early springtime will find the bass going to structure located between the deep water into the shallow water in preparation for the spawn. The fisherman has a reasonable idea of where the bass will be because of the time of year.

A deer hunter can pattern deer in much the same way. Before hunting season, deer have a normal routine they follow to and from feeding and bedding areas. Prior to the season, the hunter can search for deer in places that provide one of these two needs for the whitetail.

During the rut, the buck deer often will make scrapes and be in regions where they can breed the does. When heavy hunting pressure is present, deer generally will go to thick cover to avoid hunting pressure. Deer have preferred foods at certain times of the year that only are in season during that particular time of the year. Depending on the time of the year you hunt the whitetail, you can make some reasonable assumptions as to where the deer should be, based on the above facts. By knowing where the deer should be, you can begin to narrow down the sections of land where you look for deer.

Terrain Reduces The Amount Of Land To Hunt

The bass fisherman realizes he can't attempt to catch a bass in two inches of water, because that's not enough water for the fish to survive. He also knows that trying to get his boat into an area where the water is too shallow is pointless.

The deer hunter also can shrink his hunting region by studying the terrain he has to hunt. Although deer can and will cross openings and clearings, swim rivers or lakes or climb mountains, the terrain of the area you're planning to hunt will eliminate some of the spots where you ordinarily must look for deer.

Deer will swim rivers and lakes and cross streams when they are being pursued.

How To Use Pressure Points

Since bass flee from fishing pressure, the bass angler understands if he is to catch more and bigger fish, he must try and fish sites few other sportsmen are angling. The same is true of hunting.

The places with the most hunters often will have the fewest deer, while the areas with the least number of hunters will home the most deer. Understanding hunting pressure aids the deer hunter in decreasing the amount of woods he has to search to try and find a deer.

If a woodsman has 8,000 acres to hunt, by using this process of elimination, he may have shrunk his basic hunting region to 4,000 acres. Now he has less land to cover and has maximized his chances for taking a deer by 100 percent. But if we plan to bag deer, we must reduce that 4,000 acres by scouting down to the effective range of the shotgun or rifle with which we are hunting.

How To Scout For The Magic Half-Mile

The magic half-mile is a place in the woods where big bucks should appear. But locating that half-mile is not an easy task. Olympic athletes train in over-distance and under-distance to prepare for a race, which means they train by running further than they actually plan to run in a race, besides sprinting shorter distances than they know they will be required to run.

For our hypothetical hunt, we have an over-distance of 4,000 acres. Let's look at a shorter distance, and see if we can't learn something from the hunters who must have deer much closer than most gun hunters do -- the bow hunters. These sportsmen aren't searching for the magic half mile. They are attempting to discover the magical 30 yards.

While interviewing two of the most consistent bow hunters I know, they made the same recommendation. "There is no way to shrink the woods to a distance to where deer can be harvested without spending many hours scouting."

Clarence Yates, who has taken more than 100 deer with a bow has told me that, "Just finding a good place to hunt is not enough. To consistently bag deer, you must locate the best place to take deer each day you hunt. To do that, you have to know every tree on the property you hunt by its first name."

Dr. Robert Sheppard, one of the most meticulous bow hunters I know says, "If I have 4,000 acres to scout, I probably will have 10 to 20 stand sites. I will know which of these places will be the most productive for the time of year, the amount of hunting pressure present when I plan to hunt and the way the wind is blowing."

No shortcuts exist for learning what the magic half-mile is where you can take deer. You diligently must search for it, which is a basic key of successful deer hunting that most sportsmen completely overlook. Deer hunting is an outdoorsman's attempt to find the very best place in the woods that will provide him the greatest opportunity for seeing and hopefully bagging a whitetail. Shooting the deer is the completion of the hunt. To be an effective deer hunter, you must spend most of your time trying to find that magic half-mile to hunt.

Why Have A Half-Mile To Hunt

If you have done a careful and efficient job of scouting, you should be able to see and take a deer within a half-mile. You may have as many as four treestands in that half-mile. Then no matter which way the wind is blowing, you can come into this region and hunt.

By scouting properly, you can hunt more confidently, because then you are totally convinced you are in the very best place to take a deer. If you thoroughly understand what the deer do in that half-mile, and if you know there is a buck in that area, then your chances of success are 100 times greater than the hunter who is stumbling around in the woods hoping a deer will appear. The magic half-mile is the spot most successful deer hunters try to find, because they often can take more than one buck from a region like this and may bag deer for several years from this same half-mile -- if the terrain and habitat doesn't change.

What The Magic Half-Mile Looks Like

Although the magic half-mile will look different in various parts of the country and can be found in several types of terrain, magic half-miles have some similar characteristics. Here's a look at what has made these places so productive and why they can be hunted during an entire season and often even for several years.

A Thicket

I hunted a thicket for several years when I was in college that was in the middle of a river bottom hardwood swamp that often flooded during hunting season. This thicket was productive, because it was protected from hunters by water. The woods that flooded during the rainy season contained water oaks, white oaks, willow oaks and red oaks. The thicket was on high ground, which meant that even when the river rose, the deer had sanctuary. Inside the thicket were plentiful blackberries and greenbriar. Since there were trails leading into the water, I knew the deer had to be in the thicket.

But the problem with hunting this thicket was the water surrounding it was over chest-wader high. Finally when all else failed, I took a canoe through the woods, paddled across the water and reached the thicket. I spooked numbers of deer and could hear them run off. Occasionally I even saw the whites of their tails.

The first day or two I hunted the thicket, I was unsuccessful. However, after I spent a day scouting the thicket, which was about 1/2-mile long when the water was up, I found a break in the cover near one end of the island thicket. I soon learned if I crossed the water and took a stand near that opening well before daylight I consistently saw deer that were holding in the thicket on the island during daylight when hunting pressure was great in surrounding regions. To protect my magic thicket, I tried to make sure no one saw me going into or out of the woods when I hunted.

Many times a magic half-mile can yield bucks throughout a season and even year after year, because the region is a sanctuary the deer use to flee to from hunting pressure.

The Neck Of A Funnel

After researching why some deer hunters are successful and where they hunt, I have learned how effective hunting a funnel can be. A funnel is where the woods narrow down to a small neck -- usually with woodlots on either end of the neck and some type of habitat break surrounding the woodlot.

One magic half-mile funnel where I successfully bagged deer the last several years was made when the U.S. Army Corps of Engineers clearcut and dug out a large section of woods on the bank of the Tombigbee River near my home in Alabama. Since this large spoilage area was to be utilized for dumping the sediment dredged up from the river, it was scraped down to the bare earth. One corner of this spoilage region came within 150 yards of a clearcut. The woods between the corner of the spoilage area and the clearcut consisted of oaks that yielded many acorns.

Discovering an area like this -- if you don't know what to look for -- often can be difficult. Many times deer meander through a funnel without establishing well-used trails. However, sometimes deer on both ends of a funnel will move back and forth through a region to get from one part of the woods to the other.

In one afternoon, I counted more than 40 deer traveling through this Corps of Engineers' created funnel near the river. Until the spoilage area grew up in briars and heavy cover, this spot was a magic half-mile. Generally a funnel area consistently will be productive for a long time, unless the terrain changes.

A Half-Mile Of Food

Deer in many parts of the country have a preferred food they eat at different times of the year. Deer will come from many regions of the woods to feed on one of their favorite foods when this food is in high demand and short supply.

The typical example in my section of the country is the first white oak tree to drop its acorns. The deer will concentrate and come

The author successfully hunted a funnel area to locate one of his many trophy bucks.

from great distances to get to that particular tree and feed on those acorns. The hunter who locates the food supply tree usually can take a stand anywhere within a half-mile radius of that tree and bag deer as long as the tree continues to drop acorns. But this half-mile only may be magical for a few days or a week or two before it loses its magic -- if the spot is dependent on food or hunting pressure to concentrate the deer.

A Magic Saddle

A saddle is a low place in a mountain range that deer utilize to cross the mountains. Oftentimes if you can find a saddle in a mountain, it can become a magic half-mile hunting spot and home deer throughout hunting seasons for many years to come.

A Honeymoon Suite

In many sections of the country, deer often will make scrapes and meet does at the same places year after year, even though the buck that originally has made the scrape may have been killed. Since there is a pecking order in a deer herd, subordinate bucks know where dominant bucks scrape and meet does. A subordinate buck may have fought with a dominant buck at a particular scrape. Consequently, when the dominant buck is removed from the herd, and a subordinate buck takes the position of the dominant buck, he may scrape in the same spots and under the identical trees the previous dominant buck has. If a sportsman discovers one of these honeymoon half-miles where bucks historically have scraped, he may find a spot to harvest a buck every season for several years.

The magic half-mile is the very best place in the woods where deer will concentrate or come through during hunting season. To be a magical region, this spot must be where a hunter can stand and have a reasonable chance of bagging a deer with at least three different wind conditions so he can hunt the area without his scent being blown into his hunting place. The magic half-mile must invoke in the hunter the feeling that he is holding four aces when he is hunting over this spot. The magic half-mile consistently will produce more deer each year than any other place in the woods.

To increase your odds for harvesting a buck this season, use the suggestions to shrink the amount of woods you have to hunt. Try and pattern the deer as to the season, the food source they prefer and whether or not the buck is interested in sex at the time you want to hunt him.

Then don't be satisfied with just a good place to hunt. Find the very best part of the most productive half-mile of woods in the entire woodlot you have to hunt. Know what makes that one half-mile the most choice area. Understand how and where to put up treestands so you can hunt that half-mile no matter what the wind condition is.

CHAPTER 4

HOW TO KNOW WHEN DEER MOVE

ABOUT 90 PERCENT of the deer harvested each season are taken when the animals are moving. Rarely will a hunter find a buck bedded down and be able to bag him. Knowing when, why, where and how deer move is a critical key to deer hunting success.

One of the nation's foremost authorities on deer behavior who also regularly hunts many species of game is Dr. Karl V. Miller in the School of Forest Research at the University of Georgia. Miller explains, "Buck deer move primarily to meet their survival needs, which are food, water and shelter, to be comfortable as they respond to warmer or cooler temperatures, to avoid insects and to find and breed does during the breeding season."

An avid deer hunter for more than three decades and a teacher of bow, black powder and rifle deer schools, Ronnie Groom of Panama City, Florida, says, "Deer don't move any more than they absolutely have to, especially when hunters are in the woods. Although a preferred food source can draw deer from one area to another, I've observed the rut and the opportunity to breed causes deer to move more than any other factor."

Eddie Salter, two time World Champion turkey caller, owner of Eddie Salter Calls in Brewton, Alabama, and master woodsman, reports that, "Temperature and habitat also seem to affect deer movement. I believe southern deer don't store up as much fat in their bodies as northern deer do because of the milder winters in the South. Then when a cold front hits the South, deer move more to stay warm and find food than the deer in the North do."

Biologists have learned that one type of deer movement involves elongated patterns within a deer's home range. Deer eating a single vegetative food or two similar kinds of food move out in all directions to feed from a central point. However, deer feeding on two or more divergent types of food are more likely to move in a straight line searching for food.

Northern whitetails tend to move more and have larger and less stable home ranges than southern deer. Although the average whitetail movement generally has a radius of one to two miles, in a South Dakota study, the total range was 11.8 miles, and one adult deer moved 126.8 miles in 18 months.

Another factor affecting deer movement is population density and type of habitat. Deer in open habitats generally have large home ranges; deer in heavily vegetated areas don't move as much. For example, a Minnesota study showed that the average distance a deer moved in a coniferous forest was 5.1 miles and the greatest distance was 22 miles. However, prairie deer moved an average of 9.6 miles with a maximum movement of 55 miles.

The age and sex of deer also influences their movements; young fawns move little, whereas yearlings and young adults move over large areas. Deer decrease their wanderings as they grow older. But adult bucks usually have larger home ranges than does.

Peak Time Of Day For Deer Movement

From interviews with experts including biologists and hunters, four factors seem to be most responsible for the time of day when deer move: the amount of daylight, intensity of hunting pressure, air temperature and the reproductive cycle of the deer.

Charles DeYoung, professor of wildlife management at Texas A & I University, explains that, "In Texas where the climate is hot and the winters mild, we usually see two different types of movement. The deer seem to move during extremely hot weather and very cold weather and mainly early in the morning and late in the evening. When the temperature is mild, there doesn't seem to be any definable pattern as to when deer will move."

Miller mentions too that deer are, "Primarily crepuscular--moving at twilight and dusk. Sometimes they will move in the middle of the day, mainly to avoid hunting pressure."

In a 1970 study done in northern Michigan, the peak activity times of the whitetail deer were during December and January and then in late March when the deer were browsing. Ozoga and

When heavy snow falls, deer often will yard-up in protected areas.

Verone, biologists doing the study, found deer moved the most at four to six hour intervals at sunrise, midday, sunset and twice during the night. As winter continued, the nocturnal and early morning feeding movements were reduced, and deer moved more in the warmer parts of the day.

David Hale, one of the owners of Knight and Hale Game Calls in Cadiz, Kentucky, and a nationally recognized deer hunter, confirms this. "Especially during the rut, you see more deer from 10:00 A.M. to 2:00 P.M., which may be because the dominant buck is breeding and chasing does at night. Perhaps deer then rest during early morning hours when they know hunting pressure is the highest and move in the middle of the day after they have rested when the hunting pressure is not as intense."

How Temperature Influences Deer Movement

Some hunters believe deer move less in hot weather than they do in cold weather. However, other hunters think that extreme hot or cold temperatures cause deer to move less. Apparently severe weather changes retard deer movement rather than increasing their movement. Studies have shown that deer tend to move less in deep snow to conserve their energy. Also malnourished and weakened deer don't have the energy to move much in very cold weather.

When the North experiences extreme winter weather and heavy snow, whitetail deer congregate with other deer in sheltered places--a concept known as yarding. These groups of deer conserve energy by minimizing radiant and convection heat loss and move very little. A behavior similar to yarding often is observed in the Appalachians where deer concentrate in coves and on hillsides with mountain laurel and rhododendron cover in the winter.

But Ronnie Groom, who hunts primarily in the South, has found, "When a morning is cool, and the temperature drops below 32 degrees, deer tend to be more active than they are when the temperature is stable."

Apparently weather change can increase the amount of deer activity because David Hale observes that, "Just before a weather front comes through an area, deer seem to move more than they do once the front hits. We know deer feed heavily before bad weather. Also I believe the amount of decreasing light that accompanies shorter days is a primary factor in when deer move. I tend to see more deer moving, especially bucks, when the days are shorter than when the days are longer."

How Wind Affects Deer Movement

The wind can hide a hunter's movement. If wind remains constant, you easily can determine wind direction and stalk into the wind. Many hunters are convinced a windy day is a more productive day to hunt than a calm day.

Dr. Miller believes that on high wind days, deer often move into fields because they can't trust the sounds they hear in the woods.

To bag a buck on a windy day, consider hunting trails leading to open fields or putting on a man-drive in open fields to hopefully jump up the deer. Then you can take a shot.

Groom breaks the amount of deer movement you can expect to see into three different wind conditions. "A light wind doesn't influence deer movement at all. I believe medium wind tends to make deer bed down because their senses of smell, sight and hearing are impaired to some degree. They realize they can't detect danger as well. A heavy, blowing wind makes deer very nervous, and they may jump up and run for no reason. The deer has a difficult time

Your best bet for taking a buck on windy days may be to hunt trails.

detecting movement in a heavy wind. The deer's ability to smell is very decreased, and his ability to hear is almost non- existent. On days of heavy winds, deer usually hole up in the thickest cover to try and dodge danger."

Hale hates to hunt on windy days because he has learned, "Deer will bed down until nightfall on very windy days, since they are not nearly as vulnerable to hunters after dark."

How Rain Affects Deer Movement

Rain affects deer in several different ways. Generally deer will move more in the rain because usually hunters move less. Most sportsmen are fair weather hunters. Hunting in the rain makes you wet and miserable. However, hunting on rainy days may be an advantage because fewer hunters are in the woods.

As Miller reports, "Deer will move in a light rain. However, in a heavy rain, they will not move or else will move very little."

Hale has found that, "Deer love rain. Apparently rain makes them feel more comfortable. Deer seem to like to stand up or walk around in the rain. But if a heavy downpour occurs, deer, like humans, will seek cover."

How Hunting Pressure Affects Deer

Most hunters feel that deer know within 1-1/2 hours of the opening day of deer season that they are in trouble. Older age class bucks respond quicker to hunting pressure than younger bucks do, which is how they have become older age bucks.

According to Charles DeYoung, "Hunting pressure can cause bucks to become nocturnal. When the hunters come into the woods to pursue and take deer, deer drastically decrease their daytime movement patterns and spend most of the day in heavy cover."

James G. Teer, director of the Welder Wildlife Foundation in Texas, explains that, "Hunting pressure increases the deer's flight distance. At the Wildlife Foundation, our deer are relatively tame. You can't go out and pet them, but our deer don't have to deal with hunting pressure. When the deer at the Wildlife Foundation encounter man, they only will run about 50 yards before they stop, look back and then continue on with their daily routine.

"However, when you are hunting in an area with numbers of other hunters, a deer's flight distance increases greatly. The deer may run 200 to 300 yards before he stops to look back and tries to determine whether or not he is being pursued."

The less hunting pressure exerted on deer, the more they will move during daylight hours.

How Droughts And Floods Affect Deer

Under dry weather conditions, deer have to spend more time searching for food and water. DeYoung and Teer both agree that deer must move much more in daylight hours during dry weather.

Groom has observed that, "During any time of the year, one of the best places you can hunt, not only for bucks, but particularly for trophy bucks, is in cutover areas with thick cover. However, during drought conditions, the deer will avoid clearcuts because these open spaces most often will be extremely hot and dry.

"To see a large amount of deer movement during a drought, hunt creek bottoms or the edges of lakes and streams where the deer have to come not only for water but also for food. Creek bottoms stay more moist and produce more succulent plants than arid areas do under drought conditions."

At times flooding can be a problem in parts of the country, particularly in the South. Floods will cause deer to move from low areas to ridges to avoid the water.

How Preferred Food Causes Deer To Move

Deer are browsers and eat a wide variety of grasses, shrubs, fruits and nuts. However, deer prefer certain foods at specific times of the year, and they eat particular foods every day. If you know what these foods are, often you can bag a buck as he comes or goes from one of these preferred food sources.

Dr. Miller says, "Deer will move to feed on a preferred food source like muscadine grapes, persimmons and white oak acorns."

Teer explains that, "Although deer are browsers, they will travel across hundreds of acres to get a preferred food source like acorns."

Groom has observed that, "Deer are more active when a tree is at the peak of dropping its acorns, especially a white oak tree. When white oak acorns are falling the heaviest, you'll often see deer moving to these food trees throughout the day."

How Noise Affects Deer

The experts suggest that the type of noise a deer hears affects whether he comes or runs when he hears a sound.

DeYoung explains, "Unfamiliar noise makes the deer move either to come to you or away from you. But they quickly learn to adapt to noise that is not threatening. For instance, deer often will bed down next to a busy highway. One of the strangest effects of noise on deer I have observed is when I was at Fort Sill, Oklahoma, where deer actually bedded down on the artillery range -- even when rounds were going off. That's why I believe once deer become accustomed to a sound, it no longer frightens them."

Teer reports that, "Often if you make an unfamiliar noise and stand still, a deer actually will hunt you. The animals want to find out what is making the sound. They will approach you warily --

snorting and stomping their feet to try and make you move. Then when you do move, the deer will be gone."

Miller too has observed the actions of a deer hunting a hunter. But again he re-emphasizes that each deer is an individual and that each animal may react to noise differently. "Sometimes a tractor can pass within a few yards of a deer, and he won't run off. Or, a deer may run as soon as he spots a tractor. Often a hunter's sneaking around in the woods will scare more deer than a hunter who bumbles loudly through the brush. Deer don't like to be surprised by noise. If they are surprised, they may flee. But if a deer hears an unfamiliar sound, he may come to investigate what made that sound and to assess if that sound poses any danger to him. An interesting study from Wisconsin indicates that deer were more frightened by noise made by cross country skiers than by snowmobiles."

How The Rut Affects Bucks

The rutting season of whitetail deer is tied to the diminishing ratio of daylight to darkness, information the deer receives from its pineal gland, which measures the light and then influences through the secretion of melatonin the release of sex hormones from the deer's pituitary gland. The latitude at which a deer lives governs his time of rutting, since days become shorter with less light in the northern U. S. earlier in hunting season than in the South.

Most hunters believe that during the rut the bucks are the easiest to take because they are the most active. Groom concurs by stating, "The rut is the best time of the year to hunt bucks--except on opening day of deer season when you can catch the bucks off-guard. However, increased hunting pressure can affect deer movement adversely even during the rut. In areas with high hunting pressure, the bucks often will become nocturnal even though rutting season has arrived."

Although the rut is the time of year when bucks move the most, many sportsmen fail to realize that does move during that time also.

"The bucks are obligated by their hormones to seek out does during the rut," Miller says. "However, some does in heat also may be searching for bucks. Therefore, doe movement as well as buck movement also increases in the rut."

If you plan your deer hunt around the weather conditions, the breeding season and the other factors that affect deer movement, your odds for bagging a whitetail buck dramatically will increase.

44

CHAPTER 5

HOW MOONLIGHT AFFECTS
BUCK BEHAVIOR

THE MOON WAS FULL. The woods seemed to glow as though a lantern had been brought into a darkly lit room when I moved quietly before daylight to my treestand. Having scouted the area the day before, I was confident the buck I had spotted at the Bostick Plantation near Estill, South Carolina, would be feeding in the soybean field approximately a half-mile away as I inched up the tree with my treestand. Once I was perched in the tree, I shivered in the pre- dawn light. Although daylight seemed eternally slow in coming, finally the light of first morning melted away the earth's chocolate night color. I faintly saw the trail in front of me I had predetermined the deer had to follow to come from the soybean field to a briar thicket 50 yards behind me where I assumed he was bedding.

Having stayed up too late the night before for fellowship with Terry Hiers and Joe Bostick at the hunting lodge, I snapped back to alertness before sleep forced my eyes to close all the way. Looking again down the trail, I spotted a crown of ivory atop a fat buck. I had guessed right. The big nine point was heading for his bed. I mounted my Browning .243 and found the front shoulder of the deer with my Nikon scope. Then I gently squeezed the trigger. The buck, less than 30 yards away, crumpled in his tracks.

Even though daylight had come, the moon still shone. I knew the game plan Hiers and I had laid the night before, based on our

45

assumption that bucks generally would feed on a full moon, had paid off.

Can you determine deer movement by the amount of light the moon gives off the night before you hunt? Some hunters believe bucks feed at night on a full moon and bed down during daylight hours, which means daytime hunting for bucks is usually poor if the moon has been full the night before. Another old wives' tale is when the moon is dark or no moon shines, bucks will bed down at night and move only during daylight hours.

When I wondered if I could increase my odds for bagging a buck if I planned my hunt around the different phases of the moon, I checked with master deer hunters and scientific researchers to learn what they had observed about deer movement and moon phases.

Scientists Speak On Hunting With The Moon

According to Horace Gore, a wildlife biologist with Texas Parks and Wildlife, "From my experience, I think deer move when the moon is up. If the moon comes up at 3:00 P.M., the deer will move at 3:00 P.M. Generally deer get up and down numerous times during the night, normally moving at about two or three hour intervals. Apparently, when the moon is out all night, there is more activity among deer, which may cause them not to move in the daylight hours of the first part of the next day. When the deer hunter goes out at daylight waiting for the deer movement to begin, he won't see the normal activity of deer in the early morning and at the crack of dawn as he will if the night has been more dark. I don't even like to go deer hunting in the morning when the moon has been full all night."

Many deer hunters believe the phases of the sun and the moon affect not only deer movement but also feeding patterns. This belief has fostered the use of solunar tables which attempt to predict the times of day and night when deer may be most active.

However, according to Dr. Keith Causey, professor of wildlife science at Auburn University, in Auburn, Alabama, "No scientific studies have documented a scientifically testable correlation between moon phases and sun phases and animal or deer activity. Intuitively, many hunters and naturalists think they observe these relationships, but testing this theory from a scientific standpoint is difficult.

"But just because scientists haven't developed sophisticated enough tests to evaluate whether solunar phases affect deer

Deer seem to be far more active in daylight hours when little or no moon shines at night.

movement or not does not mean there is not or cannot be a relationship between the movement of the sun and the moon and deer activity. Much evidence suggests these relationships may exist. However, as scientists, we can't prove these relationships do exist."

Hunters Speak On The Effects Of The Moon On Deer

Dr. Bob Sheppard, who has been an avid deer hunter for more than 20 years and often hunts more than 50 days each season, keeps meticulous records on deer movement, weather conditions and

47

moon phases. He has compiled all his research into a computer program to study and analyze what he has learned in the field.

According to Dr. Sheppard, "Most hunters overlook at least two factors when trying to determine the effect of the moon on deer movement. Often the moon will be full all day long during daylight hours but rarely seen at night. If the moon is full in the daytime but not at night and doesn't give off light at night, then do the deer react to the fullness of the moon, or do they react to the darkness of the night? My experience has been when the moon is full during daylight hours and dark at night, the deer tend to not feed as much at night and seem to react as though there is no moon instead of a full moon.

"Another aspect of the moon phase/deer movement question is the amount of cloud cover present on the night the moon is full. I have observed that the day after a full moon when the night has had heavy cloud cover or rain and the light from the moon does not illuminate the woods that the deer feed and move more actively during daylight hours --just as they will if no moon shines. However, a full moon with little or no cloud cover usually means the deer will be less active during daylight hours, which makes me believe they may have fed primarily at night.

"From my records, I tend to think the more light in the woods at night, the more the deer tend to move and feed at night, and the less active they'll be in the daytime. When little or no light is in the woods at night, the deer seem to be far more active in the daytime, which makes me assume they may not have fed the night before. I believe the amount of light that occurs at night, not the moon phase, determines whether or not deer feed and move at night. I'm strongly convinced of the effects of light at night on deer. A full moon and a clear sky have the effect of turning a flashlight back on the earth while the sun is on the other side of the planet. I believe the light given off by the moon is what affects animal movement, not the geological relationship of the heavenly bodies, their gravitational pull or any of the other factors thought to have an effect. I generally won't hunt the day after a bright night, particularly if the weather is warm, because I believe the deer are less likely to be active.

"However, hunters must remember no one condition determines whether deer will move or feed more actively at night or during the daytime. Weather conditions, air temperature and hunting pressure are all critical factors that also must be considered along with the amount of light in the woods at night in determining deer movement by day or by night."

Jerry Simmons, who has taken more than 300 deer with a bow in 10 years of hunting, spends thousands of hours each season studying deer and deer movement and has made some observations about hunting according to moon phase.

"If you want to take a deer in the morning, generally the bucks will be the most active when little or no moon has been present at night. If you're planning a morning hunt and want the best odds for success, be sure that no moon or little moon has appeared the night before. If a full moon has shone the night before you plan to hunt, sleep late, and don't go to your treestand until around 10:00 A.M.

"I believe that usually when there is a full moon at night, bucks, most especially the mature, smarter bucks, tend to feed during the middle of the day. Perhaps these older bucks have learned that by feeding heavily on a full moon they can bed down before daylight and not be hungry until mid-morning or noon when most hunters are not in the woods. Although I think mid-day hunting is often the best time of the day to hunt, no matter what the moon condition, I have found I see more bucks in the middle of the day when there's been a full moon the night before I hunt.

"If you're planning to hunt in the afternoon, the worst condition you can have is a full moon, especially a full moon that comes up before the sun goes down. I've learned bucks generally feed most actively during the period of the day just before a drastic change occurs from dark to light in the morning and from light to dark in the evening. However, when the moon is full in the afternoon and remains full at night without a dramatic change between daylight and dark, deer will wait until the sun has gone down and feed totally by moonlight. Maybe deer don't receive the light signal meaning that movement is safe. Then they may not move until later in the night. A deer usually will move just before dark in the dark of the moon but not move at that time if the moon is full and bright."

Horace Gore, who is both a scientist and a dedicated deer hunter, seems to agree with Simmons' generalizations about the best times to hunt according to moon phase.

"For my hunting, I've determined I generally see more deer early in the morning and late in the evening when the moon has been dark the night before," Gore explained. "I've also learned that when the moon has been full most of the night, I tend to spot more deer from 9:30 A.M. until 4:30 P.M. in the mid-part of the day with the most light."

Another factor you often may overlook in trying to determine deer movement patterns according to moon phase is the amount of available food and the distance a deer has to travel from his bedding site to that food.

As Gore mentioned, "A hungry deer won't pay nearly as much attention to the moon as a fat deer will. If a deer must travel great distances to find food, you may see him during the early morning hours traveling back to his bedding site even though there has been a full moon all night."

Psychological Effects Of The Moon On Deer

Most of us concern ourselves primarily with moon phase and the amount of moonlight in the woods the night before we hunt. However, another determining factor of deer movement maybe the times at which the moon rises and sets. Is there a correlation between when the moon appears and disappears in the sky and deer movement?

"I believe deer movement is determined as much by when the moon appears as to how much light the moon gives off at night," Gore reported. "I think the moon may have a psychological effect on deer. When the full moon is shining, but clouds cover its light, deer still will move, even though the night is as dark as if the moon is in a dark phase. If the moon comes up at 3:00 P.M. or is up in the daytime, then I think you should hunt during that time, because I believe the deer will be active."

The Effect Of The Moon According To Location And Temperature

According to longtime deer hunter, Charles Alsheimer, who conducts deer hunting seminars throughout the eastern part of the country, location and temperature are two key ingredients which must be factored in when you're considering the effects of the moon on deer movement.

"I find the effect of the moon on buck movement depends on where you're hunting," Alsheimer explained. "If you're hunting whitetails in Texas, usually not much animal activity occurs during the day after a full moon the night before. However in the Northeast, especially North of the Mason/Dixon Line, I haven't observed that moon phase affects deer much. Providing weather conditions allow

Dr. John Lanier says deer do not carry pocket watches or solunar tables.

for deer movement, I still see deer movement during the day after a full moon in this region.

"I tend to believe temperature is much more a factor in causing deer movement than moon phase. For example, in the Northeast during hot weather, no matter what the moon phase, because of the deer's heavy coats, they won't move as much as they do during cold weather and when there are high winds."

Romance And The Moon

One of the most critical keys to when deer move is the rut. If you plan a hunt strategy according to solunar tables, deer movement patterns, the light and the dark of the moon and the times the moon appears and disappears, all the conclusions you've drawn from your moonlight studies may change when you factor in the rut.

51

According to Jerry Simmons, "When a buck is in the rut, he will be chasing does or with a doe most of the time, no matter what the moon is doing. Bucks lose much of their natural caution during the rut, which is why many males are killed during this period."

Horace Gore believes that sex drive, not moon phase, dictates when a buck moves during the rut. "If the buck is looking for an estrous doe, I don't think whether the moon is up or down matters. The buck will continue to search for an estrous doe until he finds her. I don't believe the male deer during the breeding season pays any attention to the dark or the light of the moon."

Alsheimer agreed with Gore as he commented, "The sex drive of a whitetail buck will dictate that he's on the move constantly during the rut, no matter what the moon phase. Bucks lose a lot of weight during the rut because hormone levels are so high, and they're constantly moving and stressing their bodies. They aren't operating on any kind of a system or following the moon phases. They're just helter- skelter chasing does."

No Pockets And Can't Read

Dr. John Lanier of Jachin, Alabama, one of the owners of Bent Creek Lodge, is a veterinarian who has hunted and studied deer all of his life. He's taken a large number of big bucks and consistently finds a trophy buck each season. When I asked Dr. Lanier about solunar tables and timetables for predicting deer movement, he answered not only with the wisdom of his education but also his keen eye for observation that, "Deer don't have any pockets to carry solunar charts or pocket watches. They don't know when they're supposed to be where you think they should be. Even though a solunar chart tells you when a deer should be feeding and moving, just remember, he hasn't read that same chart. He'll respond more to the rumbling in his stomach or the mating on his mind than he will consider what the moon is doing at what time of day. A buck deer is an unpredictable wild animal."

Efficient, consistent deer hunting depends on your ability to evaluate the land, the weather and the deer's desire to flee hunting pressure, feed, breed, drink, move and sleep. Studying moon phases and their effects on deer can be an effective key in helping unlock the mystery of where and when a big buck will appear. However, as scientists and hunters alike in this article agree, moon phase is not the only ingredient to be considered when you're devising your hunt plan.

CHAPTER 6

HOW MUCH HUNTING PRESSURE CAN A BUCK STAND?

"YOU BOYS YELL and holler and jump into those thick places," Adrian Hitt, the huntmaster on the Tombigbee Hunting Club, instructed the drivers. "But when you come to a downed tree or an isolated briar thicket, stop walking and hollering when you're within gun range of the thicket.

"If a big buck is in that thick spot, after about a minute, he'll come blowing out of the cover. As long as the buck can hear you and knows where you are, he'll remain in that thicket and won't come out until after you've passed by. But when you hush, and the buck isn't positive about where you are, he'll become nervous and scared. Then his nerves will force him to jump up and come out of the thicket where you can take a shot at him."

About 10 a.m. I found an isolated briar thicket. Off to the right, I heard my brother, Archie, singing out, "hootie, hootie, hootie, hootie." To the left, I heard the driving sounds of, "yodee, yodee, yodee," of my nephew, Bubba. At about 30 yards from the thicket, I held my Remington 12 gauge at the ready and stood dead still.

I waited for what seemed an eternity. As I listened to the other drivers, I still heard Hitt's instructions ringing in my ears, "If a buck's in a thicket, he's got to go -- if you stop. Wait a minute or two, and he'll come out."

As a driver, I'd gone into thick cover through the years to spook the deer out. But I didn't have much faith in this new tactic of waiting silently. However, I knew Adrian Hitt was a master deer

53

hunter who consistently bagged more bucks than any other drivers on the Tombigbee Hunting Club. So I waited. I felt foolish, but I waited. If no deer was in that briar thicket, I had wasted my time.

Just as I made the decision to begin to yell and start to walk again, the briars came alive with antlers and hooves. The buck dove straight away from me to get out of the briars. At the same time, my shotgun with No. 1 buckshot found its comfortable resting place in the hollow of my shoulder. As the buck came up again for his second jump out of the thicket, the bead on the barrel found the groove between the deer's two shoulder blades where the neck joined the body. When my gun reported, the buck went down.

As I walked over to the fat six point to admire my trophy, I wondered ...

● how I had used the fear factor to take the buck,
● what caused deer to fear man,
● how much hunting pressure could deer stand and
● how many human encounters could a deer that lived on 2,000 acres have with humans before he started avoiding an area.

Because I realized my learning more about how and why a deer reacted to hunting pressure would help me bag bucks more effectively, I talked with master hunters and scientists to find out the answers.

How Deer Learn To Fear Man

"Deer learn to fear man just like any other animal learns to fear man," Dr. Keith Causey, professor of wildlife science for the Department of Zoology and Wildlife Sciences at Auburn University in Auburn, Alabama says. "Man's been a predator, and deer has been a prey species for thousands of years. The deer that don't fear man have been weeded out of the population. Fear by prey of a predator comes from experience and from being taught by the more mature members of the population."

Dr. Bob Sheppard of Carrollton, Alabama, a master hunter, also is a cardiologist who must pay close attention to even the smallest detail when practicing medicine. This trait of his also applies to his deer hunting.

"Most hunters believe deer learn to flee from hunters when the animals see men and that deer associate sighting a man with the knowledge that man is a predator," Dr. Sheppard reports. "However, I tend to believe deer learn to fear first the odor man gives off. Then at some time during the deer's development, the animal associates that odor with a visual sighting of man.

Dr. Bob Sheppard believes deer associate human odor with man as the predator.

"As you walk through the woods, your body produces odor that smells much stronger to the deer than to you. I'm convinced deer recognize that human odor as a dangerous smell and do all they can to avoid it."

Brad Harris, Public Relations Director of Lohman's Game Calls and one of the nation's leading deer hunting authorities, explains that, "In the woods, deer are aware of all the sights, smells and sounds of the forest. When man comes into the forest, man presents an unfamiliar sight, sound and smell. Because the deer's natural instincts teach him to avoid anything not native to his environment, this may explain how deer learn to dodge hunters."

Also we know from spending thousands of hours watching deer in the wild that a tremendous amount of information is transferred from the doe to the fawn during that first year of life. If you've watched young fawns with a doe, she will communicate danger, caution, fear and calmness to her offspring.

Bob Foulkrod of Pennsylvania, a professional hunter and guide, suggests that, "Fawns learn from their mothers to run from man."

According to Dr. Causey, "Scientists have observed that initially fawns use a strategy of freezing to hide from danger until they reach five to seven days old. After that time, they flee from man or any other predator or animal that approaches them."

Dr. Sheppard feels fawns fear man, particularly in the South, because, "Bow season starts early in the fall -- often from mid-August to mid-October. In most of the areas where hunting pressure is heavy, by the time gun season arrives in November, many of the fawns, even those still with spots, have had enough encounters with human odor in the company of their mothers to recognize the smell as a danger signal. They have learned from their mothers while walking through the woods and seeing their mothers' reactions when they encounter human smell. The doe will jerk her head up, snort and run off when she and the fawn smell humans. The next time the fawns encounter the smell, they know it means danger."

How Human Contact Affects Deer Movement

Many hunters believe the more a deer sees or smells humans, the less likely that animal is to appear in the woods during daylight hours. However, Bob Foulkrod believes the intent of the human determines the fear factor of the buck. "If a buck is in a non-pressure situation where he sees hikers, blueberry pickers or photographers during the summer months, he may run on first sighting the human before turning to see if he's being pursued," Foulkrod mentions. "When he realizes he isn't being chased or shot at, he can take a lot of human pressure. But after hunting season opens, and the bucks realize that every time they come in contact with humans they will be pursued, only a little pressure will put a buck into his nocturnal state. He will cease his daytime activities -- especially if he is a 2-1/2 or 3-1/2-year old deer."

Causey agrees with Foulkrod as he states that, "Since deer are individuals, determining how much hunting pressure one deer can withstand and using that information to draw a conclusion about all deer is impossible. However, from the harvest data I've seen and the data sets I've looked at, I know that when a buck is three years old or older and experiences intense hunting pressure then he becomes reclusive in his behavior and almost impossible to harvest legally because of his nocturnal activity."

Foulkrod, pictured, believes the hunter's intent determines the deer's fear factor.

What Happens When Deer Become Nocturnal

Brad Harris is convinced there are trophy bucks on many of the nation's public hunting areas. However, he also believes bucks have learned to use the cover of darkness to hide their movements.

"The older age class bucks with several years of hunting experience know intimately the area of the woods they've lived in for many years as well as when and where hunters will appear during daylight hours, " Harris comments. "These bucks have learned more about how to pattern hunters and their movements than the hunters understand about how to pattern deer. These trophy bucks do not move where hunters are during daylight hours. They're not lying down all day but are moving in places where hunters aren't."

Sheppard agrees with Harris about Harris' observations and offers an interesting way to find and take these nocturnal bucks.

"At night when deer move through the woods, they can smell where the hunter has been all day long," Sheppard reports. "Then the older age class bucks avoid those places during daytime hours by moving into thick cover where no human voluntarily will walk.

"One of the regions where an older age class, nocturnal deer likes to stay during daytime hours is a five or six year old clearcut. You can bag these nocturnal bucks by climbing as high as you can in a treestand, which allows you to look down into a clearcut. I've

57

seen older age class bucks in these heavy cover clearcuts stand up, stretch, urinate and defecate. They may walk one or two yards before lying down again.

"With binoculars, I've been able to spot these bucks when they stand up or move their heads from side to side. These thick cover, nocturnal bucks may move only 30 yards in a 15 hour day. But, if you're high enough to look down into a thicket, oftentimes you can take these trophy bucks, even though they are nocturnal."

How Hunters Can Reduce Pressure And Increase Deer Sightings

The only way to eliminate hunting pressure is to reduce the number of hunters who hunt any given piece of property or reduce the number of times each hunter goes onto that land. However, our experts have some creative alternatives to reduce hunter pressure on the land you hunt.

Foulkrod suggests that, "If you're in a hunting club with 20 members, try and reduce that number to 10. Then fewer people will be pressuring and attempting to take the same number of deer.

"A better solution may be to hunt posted property. I don't mean you should violate the law or trespass. However, I look for posted property. Then I go to the landowner, talk to him about why he has posted his property and convince him I'm not the type of hunting slob who has caused him to put up the No Trespassing signs. Talking to the landowner may help you gain permission to hunt posted property no one else can hunt. You may find and develop a deer hunting hotspot by simply being courteous to the landowner."

Causey recommends you specify the times of day you hunt to help reduce hunter pressure. "If for instance, your hunting club imposes a rule that all hunters must be in the woods before daylight, not leave the woods until 10:00 A.M., must be out of the woods by 10:30 A. M., cannot reenter the woods until 2:00 P.M. and then must wait to leave the woods after dark, you drastically reduce the amount of hunter movement in the woods. This strategy will reduce hunter encounters with deer. I believe reducing the amount of vehicular activity and hunter activity during specific times can reduce the amount of pressure the deer feels."

Brad Harris thinks often outdoorsmen exert too much hunting pressure on the deer before hunting season opens.

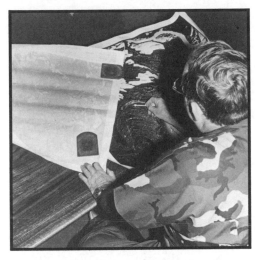

Studying aerial photos and topo maps often helps you find where trophy bucks live.

"Even scouting creates hunting pressure," Harris mentions. "When you scout the woods a week or two before hunting season, you're teaching the buck to prepare for hunting season. I do my scouting before and during the summer when the deer are in the velvet and still walking in open places. I use binoculars and try to stay as far away from the deer as I can.

"Once I've spotted the buck I want to bag, I'll wait until the week before the peak of the rut to attempt to take that deer. That's when bucks are usually moving the most and are the easiest to locate and bag. Scouting from long range reduces hunting pressure and increases your odds for bagging a buck."

What Are The Best Areas And Times To Hunt

Bucks that feel the effects of hunting pressure will hole up where deer hunters are not. If you want to take an older, trophy buck this season, study an aerial photo or topo map, and hunt five or six areas where hunters never go. These spots may include thickets, islands, a berry patch behind a hunting lodge, the edge of a road leading to camp, a little shelf off the edge of a cliff or a swamp filled with thigh-high water.

"Once you understand where to hunt, determining the best time is relatively easy," Foulkrod says. "Deer know most hunters hunt from daylight to 11:00 A.M. and from 2:00 P.M. until an hour before dark. The prime time to hunt a buck that has dodged other hunters is in the middle of the day and during the last daylight hour."

Causey relates a story of a colleague who has developed a simple method which has produced bucks for him in high pressure areas. "My hunting friend lets everyone on the lease he hunts decide where they prefer to hunt each morning. After everyone else has picked out the 'good places,' he goes to the worst hunting spots left. He often bags better bucks in these areas because these animals haven't received much hunting pressure."

Sheppard prefers to hunt high pressure bucks the last week of the season. "Before bow season, I cut shooting lanes, two to three feet wide and 10 to 25 yards long inside each thicket. Then the last week of the season, I move into these thickets with a favorable wind and watch the shooting lanes. By this time, the older age class bucks have to be in the thickets to survive. If they're there, sooner or later they have to cross those shooting lanes. When they do, I bag them."

How To Prevent Bucks From Seeing, Smelling Or Hearing You

According to Causey, "To prevent deer from seeing you, reduce the speed at which you move. Motion is what deer pick up more than anything else. Camouflage clothing is necessary to reduce the human outline. However, reduction of motion will help prevent your being detected. To prevent deer from hearing you, wear soft clothing, and be careful where you step. To keep deer from smelling you, stay downwind of the animal. I have little faith in chemicals that supposedly mask human odor from whitetails."

Often the best hunter in the woods is the trapper, since he leaves the least amount of human scent, moves through the woods like a shadow and spooks very little game. Studying how trappers go through the woods to remain undetected will aid deer hunters in being more successful.

Wearing thigh-high rubber boots means far less odor from not only your feet but also your legs. If you can wade a small creek or a branch to get to your stand, you make less noise, leave less scent and come from a direction that deer are not expecting. Move into the woods before daylight and come out after dark. If you stay in your treestand more and walk less, the likelihood of spooking deer and seeing more deer is greatly increased.

When you're hunting high pressure bucks, the more you reduce the chances of a deer seeing, smelling or hearing you, the greater your odds will be for bagging that buck of a lifetime.

CHAPTER 7

HOW EFFECTIVE ARE SCENTS?

EACH DEER SEASON thousands of hunters bag their bucks by using deer lure, which is why the scent business has experienced a boom in recent years. But also every year, thousands of other outdoorsmen swear deer lures don't work and accuse the people who buy this magic in a bottle as being as gullible as the frontiersmen of old who purchased snake oil from traveling salesmen.

Will deer lure work for you? Can you trust the ingredients in a bottle to do what the manufacturers say they will do? Will you increase your odds for bagging a buck by buying and using deer lure this season?

We tried to answer these questions when we gathered information from a distinguished panel of experts from across the nation. Our experts included Mike Cartwright, forest wildlife biologist of Arkansas Game and Fish in Mountainview, Arkansas; Bruce Whitman, chief of the Division of Information, Pennsylvania Game Commission in Harrisburg, Pennsylvania; Dr. Larry Marchinton, professor of wildlife biology, School of Forest Resources, University of Georgia, Athens, Georgia; Lee Christianson II of Eleva, Wisconsin, an avid deer hunter and consultant for Wellington Outdoors, the makers of Tink's and Ben Lee's; Brian Johansen, director of advertising for Buck Stop in Stanton, Michigan, and Linda Robbins Leasher, president of Robbins Scents in Connellsville, Pennsylvania.

Do Scents Attract Bucks?

Before purchasing any type of deer lure, ask whether or not a product in a package or a bottle actually causes deer to come to you.

"Yes, deer lures do bring in deer," Lee Christianson says. "Deer want to investigate anything they don't understand. If deer notice a new smell, they don't run the other way unless they perceive danger. If they smell an odor like another deer they are unfamiliar with or an odor that has a distinctive food base and no alarm stimulus is associated with that smell, they will approach from the downwind side. This curious nature of deer has been documented and proven."

Wildlife biologist Mike Cartwright agrees with Christianson that, "Scent communication is very important to deer. They communicate through their sensory perceptions using various organs in their body. I certainly think scents do affect deer, and I believe deer do react when a hunter uses scents. Scents can attract deer to a particular site under certain circumstances."

Bruce Whitman is somewhat more cautious as he explains that, "Scents seem to work, and I've used them myself. Scents are probably just a part of the overall picture of more specialization in hunting today. 20 years ago hunters just picked up their guns and went hunting. But, today more time and effort are put into hunting."

According to Linda Robbins Leasher, "I'm convinced scents work. No matter what lure or scent you put out -- a sex lure or any other type--the deer's curiosity will get the best of him when he smells another animal, and he will come in if he picks up that scent."

Brian Johansen also states strongly that, "If scents are properly used, they will bring in deer."

Dr. Larry Marchinton, who has studied deer behavior as his livelihood all his adult life, reports, "Sometimes deer lures will work. But luring in bucks is very complicated. The ability of a lure to bring in a buck depends on the lure itself, the sex and age class of the deer and where the deer is at in his reproductive cycle."

From our panel of experts, we've learned that deer lures can work but variables enter into when and if lures work.

What Causes Deer Lure To Work

Not all deer lures are created equal, and some may be more effective than others.

Dr. Marchinton tries to judge cautiously why lures work when he states, "Lures will work sometimes. Often I think deer react

Deer lure often is most effective in areas where least used.

more out of curiosity than anything else. They may be responding to a strange scent in their environment. So many different kinds of scents are on the market, I have no way of knowing what's in them. I'm not going to judge any particular scent as good or bad."

Mike Cartwright mentions that, "During the breeding season, the communication between the bucks and does is very strong. That's why the behavior pattern of a buck changes, and he begins to make scrape lines and deposit scent through urine over his tarsal glands on his hind legs. The urine mixes with the scent on the tarsal gland, leaves a very strong smell and communicates information to other deer in the area -- both does and bucks. The bucks can tell by the scent a doe leaves whether or not she is receptive to breeding during the breeding season. Scent communication is much more developed in deer than in humans."

Lee Christianson explains that, "Basically lures are either a sex lure, which initiates a breeding response, a food lure, which calls deer to eat or a curiosity lure, which stimulates a deer to come and investigate. You've heard the old saying that curiosity kills the cat. I believe curiosity has killed more deer than it has cats. Deer are gregarious herd animals and very social. They want to meet and greet new individuals in their herd."

What Types Of Lures Work Best

Although the experts tend to agree that hunters should use the scents and lures they have the most confidence in, a number of variables determine which lure works best. According to Marchinton, "All lures have a place in the overall scheme of hunting, but the hunter must have confidence in and be comfortable with the lure he's using. Some scents undoubtedly do attract deer at certain times. At other times, those same scents may scare off deer.

"For instance, if you utilize a dominant buck scent, and a young buck comes in to it, the younger buck may feel he must get out of that area once he has identified the scent. The effectiveness of specific scents on individual deer seems to be a matter of the deer's rank or position in the herd, what kind of animal that scent or lure was made from and the quality of the scent being used. One of the ways I define quality is, how well has that scent been preserved? Numbers of scents are on the market, but I'm not sure how good they are."

Lee Christianson explains, "I prefer to use the sex kinds of lures -- either the dominant buck lures or the doe lures. If you can introduce the smell of a new buck or a new doe into a buck's environment, I believe he'll come to investigate."

Like Christianson, Brian Johansen states he is a firm believer in the power of sex lures. "But, by using a combination of sex scents and territorial scents, you can put out a powerful calling card for bucks. When you use a territorial scent and a sex scent in combination, I feel the buck reacts like a man who comes home and smells a different after-shave lotion than he uses in his bedroom. He will be curious and go looking for the intruder."

Bruce Whitman believes that for scents to be effective, you must match the scents to the time of year you are hunting and the amount of hunting pressure in an area.

"For example at the beginning of archery season, deer aren't in full rut mode. So you may not want to use a sex scent at this time of the year. You may want to choose a different type of scent. If you are hunting in a high pressure region on opening day of deer season, and everybody in the woods is putting out some type of deer lures, then any deer lure probably will be counterproductive because of the large amount of lure being put out by the hunters."

From my own experience, I've learned that deer lure works best in areas where it is rarely used. I've observed that the more deer lure utilized in a particular place, the more ineffective that lure is. Because deer come to investigate a new and different smell, if everyone hunting a piece of property is using the same deer lure and deer smell that lure frequently, then that particular lure becomes unproductive. A new lure introduced into a region seems to draw in more bucks than a lure often utilized in the same area. From my own observation, I believe that perhaps the most productive lure when you are hunting is a lure no one else is using in an area where few others are hunting.

How A Buck Lure Brings In A Buck

Can a scent or a lure discriminate according to the sex of the animal it calls? Can we say a buck lure will bring in only bucks? When we posed this question to our team of experts, Lee Christianson responded with, "Bucks can be stimulated in two different ways -- to defend their breeding areas and to breed.

"Some buck lures give off the scent of a dominant buck. When a dominant buck in an area smells the odor of another dominant buck, he wants to find the intruder and drive that other buck out of his breeding site. A dominant buck lure like the Intruder Tarsal Gland from Wellington Outdoors is a product that can bring in bucks. A gland from a dominant buck is packaged with a separate container of buck urine. Then the hunter pours buck urine on the gland to activate it. The deer urine mixes with the lipids on the tarsal gland and makes a musky type derivative that gives off a specific rutting odor. The theory behind this kind of buck lure is the hunter is trying to create the smell of a dominant buck that has wandered into another dominant buck's territory to possibly breed the does there. Utilizing this type of lure should call in a dominant buck to defend his territory.

"The other school of thought on buck lures is to use a scent of a doe that is ready to breed. To make this scent, a doe tarsal gland and doe urine are mixed to give off the smell of a doe in estrus. If a buck never has smelled this particular doe before, he may think a new doe has wandered into his region and that she is ready to breed.

He believes this doe is not from the core family group in his area. This type lure works because it plays on two of the deer's emotions -- his sex drive and his curiosity. The buck wants to know where this doe has come from, who she is and if she's receptive to breed."

Bruce Whitman reports that, "Most buck lures may be a misnomer. A buck lure probably contains hormones a doe will give off when she's ready to mate or getting ready to mate. These hormones attract the buck because of his natural mating instincts."

Mike Cartwright thinks buck lures can work, depending on what's in them. "Bucks are not necessarily territorial, but they are defensive during the breeding season. The scent posts or scent markings deer make in the woods communicate to the bucks and/or to the does that another buck is in the area."

Larry Marchinton believes that, "Many things are labeled buck lures. If the tarsal scents are made from tarsal glands and if that scent is representative of the actual smell of a deer, then we think this lure can communicate the individuality of the animal. That scent may be able to communicate the sex of the animal that has produced the scent. We strongly suspect that the scent probably even communicates the social position or rank of that deer in the herd. This theory is not proven and is not scientific fact. Biologists only have some circumstantial evidence to support this idea."

When Scents Don't Work

Scent manufacturers and proponents of utilizing scents will lead you to believe that any time you use a deer scent or a deer lure you can draw in a wall-hanging buck. However, scents are ineffective at certain times and under particular conditions.

As Dr. Marchinton reports, "Scents may or may not work at any time. Biologists don't know how scents are carried. But under certain conditions, scents travel better. I don't think anybody fully understands when that is. If the air is dry, scents may not travel very well. Too, wind patterns will be a factor in how well scents travel. However, at particular times, scents seem to rise and travel through the air better than at other times. I believe humidity and wind are key factors affecting how effective scents are."

Another problem with scents that can cause them not to work is when hunters use one inappropriate for a certain time of the year.

Linda Robbins Leasher explains that, "One common mistake hunters make is using doe-in-heat lure during the pre-rut. Some

A dominant buck lure may bring in a dominant buck like this one.

hunters don't know how to correctly use scents, and then the scents don't work for them.

"Our company recommends you never put a scent on your body or your clothing. Always place the scent in the area you want to draw the deer to, like a bush or a tree. Never put the scent on the bare ground or in a region that if the buck approaches, you can't see him. You also must eliminate your human odor when and where you are putting out scent, or else the deer lure will be ineffective."

Knowing when the deer is in its reproductive cycle can be critical to deer lure selection. As Mike Cartwright says, "Probably any type of scent will be less effective outside of the breeding season."

Lee Christianson reports that, "A sex scent obviously will not work when a buck is not in his reproductive cycle. Also the most effective time for a buck lure to bring in a buck is the first time the animal is exposed to the lure.

"A common mistake hunters make when using deer lure is to pour buck lure on the ground and leave that lure out all night, which means the lure is working all night long pulling in nocturnal deer. But when deer go to that region and smell the lure, they will walk off because nothing is there except the smell. The next time you pour out that same lure in that same area, the buck won't respond. The best way to use deer lure is to only put it out during the hours you are hunting and take the lure with you when you leave."

A Magical Cure-all?

If you use a lure, are you certain to bring in a buck, as many of the ads promise? Our experts agree that no one can guarantee anybody anything concerning wild animals.

"Scents and lures are hunting tools to be used with hunting skills to bag your buck," Linda Robbins Leasher mentions. "If scents and lures are used improperly, they can cause you not to see your buck. However, if lures and scents are utilized properly, they can enhance your chances of bagging bucks. Besides the element of luck involved in hunting, many hunters forget that each deer is an individual with its own personality and mood which means each deer will respond to various things at different times."

Brian Johansen advises us that, "Scents are just another useful tool for deer hunting. At times, scents will work very effectively but not at other times -- no matter which you use. However, when a buck comes to the spot where that attractant is and spends 10 seconds smelling it, then the scent or lure has given you the opportunity to bag that buck by bringing the deer to the spot and giving you time to shoot. What more can you ask of any product?"

Another advantage to using scents and lures is, "Scents allow you to distract the animal's attention away from you to another area so often you can get a shot," Lee Christianson says. "One of the problems associated with hunting in high pressure areas is the deer often will spot you in a treestand. However, if the deer comes in smelling the lure, he will focus on the site where the smell is coming from instead of looking up in the trees for you. Then you have the opportunity to move and get into position for the shot without the deer's ever seeing you. A deer focused on a scent and trying to

Terry Rohm uses a doe tarsal gland to lure in bucks.

determine where it is coming from usually will be standing still or moving very slowly, which will present you with a clean, easy target."

From these scientists, expert hunters and lure manufacturers, we have learned that scents and lures can and will work if used properly and at the right times of the year. However, scents, lures or any other hunting aid will not always produce a buck on every hunt. Often we expect too much out of the equipment we use. But, every hunting aid has its advantages. On particular days at certain times, deer lures and deer scents can be the key to your success in bagging a buck.

CHAPTER 8

WHY BUCKS FIGHT

THROUGH THE RIVER bottom cane, I saw two bucks pushing and straining against each other. Their antlers clattered as they shoved each other to establish dominance. Two spikes and three does stood back and watched the drama being played out.

I couldn't see which fighting buck was the bigger, even through my Nikon rifle scope. As quickly as the fight had begun, the hostilities stopped. The herd trotted back into the dense, three year old clearcut from where they had come before I could get off shot.

On my first hunt on White Oak Plantation near Tuskegee, Alabama, I had spent the entire first day scouting for a place to hunt. I found a region where a clearcut was divided from a hardwood creek bottom by a small, cleared firebreak. When I walked down the firebreak, I saw enough deer sign to convince me they were traveling back and forth from the clearcut where they apparently were bedding, into the hardwoods where I assumed they were feeding.

The next morning before daylight, I walked into the area where I had decided to take a stand. Just before the sun came up, I spotted a deer about 80 yards from my stand. Using my binoculars, I realized the deer was a doe.

As I watched, a whitetail parade began. After the first doe, two more does crossed the firebreak. Then a spiked buck with a flattened or palmated left antler appeared as did a second spike with antlers about five inches above the hairline. A wide-racked buck darted across the opening followed by a second, well-antlered buck.

After the two large bucks fought, and I failed to get off a shot, the deer left the area.

Sitting in the cool morning air, I decided if I didn't see another deer all day, I'd still had a very profitable hunt watching the four bucks and seeing the two larger ones fight. But within five minutes, I looked back down the firebreak and watched the flat-horned spike followed by the rest of the bucks and does go by on parade again on the same course they'd taken earlier in the morning and move into the cane along the creek bottom. However, I didn't take a shot because I still was unsure how many points the two biggest bucks had. At White Oak Plantation, you only could harvest eight point or better bucks. I didn't want to make a mistake.

The deer moved down the bank of the creek just on the other side of the cane from me. As the deer came to about 40 yards from my stand, the flat-horned spike stepped out first. He was cautious as he moved out into the hardwoods and began to feed on acorns. The three does were behind him, and the second spike followed.

I had my rifle on my knee looking at the deer through my scope when I saw a well-racked buck step into the clearing. Before I took the shot, a second, even bigger, buck came out of the cane. They were both nice eight points. However, before I could get off a shot, the two bigger bucks locked antlers and began to push and shove each other across the clearing. I watched the fight through my scope; finally the biggest buck pushed the smaller buck's nose down to the ground and held him there until the crosshairs in my scope came to rest on the biggest deer's neck. I touched the trigger of my 30/06, bringing the fight to a deadly end.

The smaller buck jumped up quickly after I downed his larger rival. I bolted the gun hastily and brought the crosshairs to rest on the second eight point's shoulder. As the smaller buck looked at his fallen rival, I said to myself, "I could take you, but I won't."

Next I moved the crosshairs to the neck of the flat-horned spike and said, "I could take you, but I won't."

Then I took deadly aim on the remaining spike and knew that I also could have bagged him. However, I lowered my rifle without ever firing a shot and watched as the bucks and the does walked back into the cane, across the firebreak and returned to the clearcut.

In one morning, I had seen two buck fights, bagged a nice eight point and could have shot at three more bucks, if the season and bag limits had permitted. This day was one of the most memorable I ever

Bucks often will spar prior to the rut to establish dominance.

spent in the woods. This day's happenings also triggered my quest for knowledge about why bucks fight.

I learned that bucks fight generally at two different periods of the year, during the pre-rut, which is before the breeding season, and in the rut, which is the breeding season. My quest for knowledge took me to some of the nation's leading scientists and hunters.

Pre-Rut Fights

Dr. Harry Jacobson, a professor in the Department of Wildlife and Fisheries at Mississippi State University, explains that, "Some buck fighting takes place all year round. A dominance order begins to become established immediately after birth. As six month old fawns mature, a pecking order starts to take shape. Most of the fighting, if there is any fighting at this time, involves a flailing of hooves or aggressive posturing initially until the bucks get their first sets of antlers. Once the bucks' antlers are hardened, fighting can occur in the more traditional manner with which we're familiar.

"I've seen some full-fledged, down-and-out, knock-out battles between mature bucks before the rut. In fact, about the time bucks rub out of velvet, some sorting out of dominance occurs which may prevent combat later on in the season when the rut arrives.

"But generally, the bucks are just basically playing in the pre-rut. When bucks spar, they are testing one another, and they're also sharpening their fighting skills without getting into full-fledged

73

combat. Much of this sparring is similar to what a father and his son do when they're fooling around. Often an older buck and a younger buck will spar, and the older buck will allow the younger buck to test himself. Younger bucks begin to spar as soon as they come out of velvet as part of their maturing process. They're learning the behavior that will at some point in the future be significant to them either in breeding or not breeding."

Terry Rohm has studied deer behavior as an active hunter most of his life. "From what I've observed in the field watching bucks before the rut, sparring is a way bucks feel each other out," Rohm reports. "Aggressive fighting doesn't really take place but rather is a push/shove match. The bucks know they've got antlers on their heads, and they're building up their necks for the rut. Or, they may be brothers or have lived with each other for most of their lives. Sometimes a push/shove match resembles a couple of kids playing."

David Nelson, district wildlife biologist for the Game and Fish Division of Alabama's Department of Conservation, observes that, "Although bucks start to spar early in the season, the fight is not a fierce one for dominance, but often dominance plays a role in it. Some sparring goes on as soon as the bucks have hard antlers. As testosterone levels begin to increase, the deer's velvet is shed, the antlers begin to get hard, and the bucks will spar."

Young bucks are like young boys in the first grade who begin to push and shove to set up who is the toughest one in the class. Oftentimes, once that dominance order is set up in the youngsters, whoever establishes himself as the toughest one of the bunch will maintain that position until the completion of elementary school.

According to Jacobson, "If a young buck is whipped one time, he is less likely to challenge again. Probably this influences the psychological part of dominance among bucks as much as actual physical size or antler size does."

Once that dominance order is set up after the bucks come into hard antlers, then the likelihood of sparring and buck fights may tend to decrease slightly.

As Nelson explains, "When dominance is established, actual fighting may subside. If a buck has been defeated by another buck, the subdominant buck may move on to another place when the dominant buck steps toward him with an aggressive posture."

Jacobson states that bucks go through a series of aggressive posturing steps before a conflict occurs. "A buck demonstrates

Author John Phillips witnessed a buck fight and bagged the biggest of the two animals.

dominance primarily through body language. When he approaches a subordinate animal, he'll usually give that animal a hard stare. If the animal doesn't then display the appropriate submissive behavior or posture, the confrontation intensifies to a whole series of displays that can end up in a buck fight."

When the dominant buck demonstrates aggressive behavior, then the challenger has to make a decision of whether to duck his head and prepare for a charge or tuck his tail and prepare to run.

Michael Stickney, senior fish and wildlife technician with the Bureau of Wildlife for the Department of Environmental Conservation at the Wildlife Resource Center in Belmont, New

York, reports, "Most of the time from what I've seen and what I've read, the dominant buck just doesn't have to fight unless there's another deer that's his equal. Usually a dominant buck will assume an aggressive posture -- lying his ears flat along his neck and walking sideways very stiff-legged with all hairs standing erect--and totally intimidate the other buck."

Battles Of Passion

When the doe comes into heat, she'll only stand to be bred for a little more than 24 hours. During that time, the bucks that want to breed her often will be in conflict.

"The most intense fighting occurs during the breeding season," Terry Rohm says. "Since does only come into heat for about 28 hours, all the bucks in an area will be fighting over that one particular estrous doe, and they'll be extremely aggressive."

Charles DeYoung mentions that, "The males will have arranged themselves in a dominant hierarchy in the summertime and early fall before the rut, which is when they become very aggressive. By the time the breeding season starts, each buck recognizes how he fits into the pecking order and doesn't have to fight to establish relationships with the others. However, the most vicious fights happen between two equally matched bucks that don't know each other and haven't worked out their dominance relationship."

This situation often occurs when bucks expand their home ranges during the rut. A dominant buck may move into another buck's home range while following an estrous doe. Current research tends to indicate that when a doe is in estrus, she often makes a journey outside her home range to find a buck to breed, which may be nature's way of preventing inbreeding. But when she leaves her home range, the dominant buck in that region may follow her. Then when she encounters the dominant buck of another area, the two bucks will have to face each other. Sometimes a fight may develop.

According to Dr. Larry Marchinton, "There is such a thing as super-dominance. A buck may be dominant anywhere he goes, if that buck is head-and-shoulders bigger and stronger than any buck in the entire area. Also some dominant bucks may not be clearly superior over each other. If a doe is in heat, and both bucks are present, they may have a dominance fight to settle which is strongest and can claim the right to breed."

The most intense fights often are between two equally matched bucks.

Even the skinniest guy on the beach will challenge the most muscle-bound bully when a woman and sex are involved. Deer exhibit similar behavior. During breeding season, even bucks on the lower end of the pecking order may challenge the dominant buck.

According to Bob Zaiglin, wildlife manager of Harrison Limited in Texas, "Though very few small bucks try to fight older bucks, this situation happens. Older bucks tend to fight other older bucks, and these bucks are more likely to really hurt each other."

However, some younger or subordinate bucks don't fight fairly in their eagerness to fight. A younger buck may run in and gore an older buck that is locked in combat with another mature buck.

"During the rut, bucks aren't sparring but are actually fighting with the intent of doing in their rival and breeding a doe," Jacobson explains. "The bucks seem to form an aggressive territory surrounding a doe in estrus. This aggressive territory is the distance that no other buck can come into without encountering antlered resistance.

"Sometimes bucks fight to the death but usually not. What wildlife scientists see more frequently is two bucks fighting, and a third, usually a subordinate buck, coming in and doing in one of the

77

two in combat while the two bigger bucks are antler to antler. Although this subordinate buck sees his chance to get into battle, as soon as the older buck squares off on him, he will run. Probably this is why rattling works. When two bucks fight, a subordinate buck realizes a doe in estrus is somewhere, and he can get a quick lick in on one of the two dominant bucks while they are locked in combat."

Duels To The Death

Most battles to the death take place among older age class bucks when the buck/doe ratio is evenly divided.

"Bucks do fight to the death but most of the time not by choice," Terry Rohm says. "Often their antlers are locked, and they're unable to get them apart. The bucks either starve to death, or one deer may break the other's neck. A buck fight usually doesn't last a long time. If their antlers don't lock, the fight only will last maybe one minute because the bucks will be very aggressive."

Dr. Hilburn Hillestad reports that, "Some research tends to indicate that when bucks move into the older age classes, they often fight so much during the rut, their bodies are so beat up, and their wounds so severe that they die when the rut is over."

"Sometimes bucks are so injured they can't survive a fight," David Nelson reminds us. "I've heard accounts of bucks locking horns and either one or both animals starving to death or one breaking the other's neck. Bucks with broken tines or main beams broken in combat are not uncommon, since bucks fight hard and often hook each other. If bucks get hit just right in a vital spot, the blow can be fatal."

A buck in the rut is highly unpredictable and dangerous, even if the buck is in a pen and is a family pet. Never enter an enclosure or attempt to pet or even get close to a tame deer when the rut occurs.

Fake Fights

Most of us have learned if we can simulate a buck fight, we often can call in a buck. Rattling antlers can produce the sounds bucks make when they're sparring or fighting a battle for dominance.

According to David Nelson, "Whether antler rattling will be productive depends not on the time of year but on the buck/doe ratios where you're hunting. Using rattling antlers is most effective in areas that have fairly even buck/doe ratios. In sections where older bucks have been eliminated through hunting, hunters probably will be unproductive in trying to lure subdominant bucks in to a

Rattling antlers during the rut can bring in a buck, like this one held by Craig Hawkins.

fight. If there is competition for available does in estrus, then right before or during the peak of the rut is an optimum time for rattling antlers."

Jacobson, who agrees with Nelson, defines the time during the rut when rattling is most effective as, "The week before and the week after the peak of the rut, particularly the week before. However, attempting to lure in a buck with rattling antlers if no older bucks are in an area to begin with is very ineffective."

Terry Rohm believes weather conditions also are key factors in effective antler rattling for luring in bucks.

"The best time for rattling antlers is a clear, crisp, cold morning because the sound of the antlers will carry far," Rohm advises.

"Rattling on windy or rainy days is not as effective. Usually a couple of weeks before the breeding season starts, bucks will set up their territories when a few does are coming into heat. When a buck hears the rattling antlers, he thinks two bucks are fighting over a doe in heat, which will bring the buck in to the sound.

"When you're rattling, you also should use cover scents like Ben Lee's Cedar Cover, Earth Cover or Pine Cover scents or Tink's Red Fox-P or Stink Skunk scents since often a big buck will circle downwind from the rattling to confirm with his nose what he's heard with his ears. Too, put out a buck lure or doe urine. If the buck gets downwind and smells a hunter instead of what he believes to be other deer, he will not come in to a region.

"How you rattle depends on the area you're hunting. If you're on property that doesn't hold numbers of big, mature bucks, you won't need to rattle often. Terrain is another factor; if the cover is very thick, rattle, and use a grunt call more often. If you can't see 100 yards, and you don't know what's in front of you, rattle more often in very short intervals, with maybe 30 or 45 seconds between rattles. Then stop and wait 15 minutes before repeating the sequence. In open terrain, you don't have to rattle nearly as much.

"Also rattling will be least effective after the rut is over. The majority of deer don't want anything to do with a fight because they are tired and run-down."

To effectively rattle in bucks, remember that deer often use more than one of their senses to confirm what they believe to be true. For instance, if a deer hears antlers crashing, many times he will want to hear other sounds that prove a fight actually is taking place. A grunt call when you rattle may make the difference in your success.

But even if the deer hears antlers clashing and grunts, he still may move in downwind to try and smell either the estrous doe the bucks are fighting over or the strong urine smell of dominant bucks that have urinated on their tarsal glands. Often hunters who utilize scents and lures in combination with rattling antlers and grunt calls will be the most successful during a fake fight.

If you understand why bucks fight and simulate the sounds a buck hears when a fight is taking place, you may be able to call more bucks to you this hunting season.

CHAPTER 9

THE WEATHERMAN CAN HELP YOU HUNT BETTER

"THERE'S A BAD winter storm headed our way that should arrive late tomorrow night," the TV weatherman said.

I was warm and comfortable sitting in my easy chair listening to the crackle and pop of the oak logs in my fireplace.

"This may be one of the worst storms of the season," the weatherman advised. "So be sure your outside water pipes are protected and that you have plenty of antifreeze in your car before tomorrow night."

My wife commented as she walked into the room, "I guess we'd better stock up on groceries tomorrow to prepare for the storm. The children may not have school. And we'd better bring the dog in to the basement."

"Those are all good ideas," I answered with a little smile. "But I'm going deer hunting tomorrow."

With a look of disbelief, anger and finally frustration, my wife said, "Deer hunting! Have you lost your mind? Didn't you hear the TV weatherman predict that the worst storm of the year is coming. Besides having to survive the cold, ice and snow, if the roads are closed, you may not get back home if you go deer hunting."

As most sportsmen know, often wives and hunting don't mix. However, my wife understands how important deer hunting is to me. As soon as the next log slipped off the pile in the fireplace and was caught by the grate, she looked up and commented, "I'll have to pack you some really warm clothes and plenty of hot coffee. You will be careful, won't you, and drive slowly?"

Before Bad Weather

I am convinced that when the Good Lord made critters He installed a weather radio somewhere in their brains. Most wildlife -- including animals, birds, fish and yes, even man -- gathers food and feeds just ahead of bad weather. And many outdoorsmen have found that the very best time to attempt to bag a buck is just ahead of a harsh winter storm during rutting season.

We all know that big bucks move a great deal during the rut because they have to find and breed the does that are in estrus. If a winter storm also is moving the deer's way, the big bucks have two reasons, instead of one, to be traveling. Usually bucks face very little peril during this time, because of the hunter's movement patterns with the coming of a winter storm. The large volume of work an outdoorsman must do around the house to prepare for a severe storm usually prevents him from hunting. Also there is the threat of being stranded on the highways or in the woods and there are more convenient days to hunt than the day before a storm hits.

In most areas, hunting pressure will be extremely light or non-existent, 12 to 24 hours ahead of a storm. The old, smart bucks that have survived many seasons of eluding the hunter understand this phenomenon. Therefore, they move, feed, and breed ahead of major winter storms. Some of the largest bucks I have killed have been bagged just ahead of a storm.

All hunting tactics like still hunting, stalk hunting, and treestand hunting will and do pay off before storms. However, the most effective technique for me is a combination of stalk and still hunting which I have named target hunting.

To target hunt effectively, you must define the target areas the bucks are most likely to be in as a storm approaches. If the weatherman tells you the approximate hour the storm will hit, you can adjust your targets accordingly by trying to think like a deer.

If you have 12 daylight hours to hunt before a storm, you can lay out a target schedule similar to this. Twelve to 14 hours before a storm, the buck has plenty of time to breed, feed and bed before bad weather sets in to stay. I believe the buck's mating instinct will supersede his need to feed or find shelter.

If you know where to find bucks during bad weather, often you can bag a trophy like this.

In this first part of my hunt day, I will be anticipating meeting Ole Mossy Horns in a scraping area, on trails leading to scraping regions, in fields where I have observed a large number of does or in other places does tend to frequent. I stalk very quickly and slowly into these spots, making sure the wind is in my face so my scent will not be carried into the area I plan to hunt. I may spend only 20 to 45 minutes and then move to another feeding area if I don't spot a deer.

Accurately predicting the very hour when a storm will strike is difficult. However, during the last one to three hours before a storm rolls in, I try to hunt bedding areas or trails leading to bedding places. I have pre-determined the regions I plan to hunt and have carefully mapped out my targets. On this last circuit of my target hunting route, I make certain that my bedding targets follow a route that will lead me back to my truck or camphouse in time to find shelter before the storm. Because like the deer, I must have shelter before the storm hits or within the first hour or two of the storm.

I also assume that if I bag a buck just before the storm that I may have to field dress the animal and leave him in the woods until the next morning. I always carry flagging tape to mark the trail and to help me find my way back to the buck the next day -- if I take him at one of my last target areas.

During Bad Weather

One certain fact about deer hunting is that no fact is always certain. However, I have determined I take fewer deer during a major winter storm than I do before or after a storm. For that reason if I don't get to hunt ahead of a storm front, I usually listen to the weatherman and plan a hunt after the weather breaks. But since there are no absolutes in deer hunting, in past years when I only have been able to arrange to hunt during a storm, I have taken deer. However, the only pattern or target area that is somewhat reliable is to hunt heavy cover to attempt to locate a buck in the bed. Most of the time the deer have spotted me before I have seen them. A good shot will be rare.

After A Storm

As soon as the weatherman reports that, "Tomorrow the storm will break, and the skies will clear," I head for the woods. These words should act like a green light to hunters and cause them to be sitting on their stands first thing the following morning. I have discovered most of the deer's heavy feeding and moving activity seems to take place for only a few hours after a storm. Although deer move more after a storm passes than during bad weather, they still are not as active as they have been immediately before the storm occurs.

Deer move frequently after a storm.

Consider two other factors -- if the moon is bright and the weather clears at night, the deer may get up and start to feed under the bright moon. If the deer do feed at night after the storm has passed, often they will bed down before daylight and not feed again until mid-day. Listen to the weatherman to learn when the storm will leave the area you plan to hunt.

Also check to see what phase the moon is in and how bright the night may be. Often we completely forget that deer carry on many of the same activities at night they do during the daylight hours. So when trying to put together a daytime hunt plan, don't disregard the effects of the weather on deer at night.

On A Bluebird Day

"The skies will be clear, the sun will be bright, and the temperature should be about normal," the weatherman said on the six o'clock news.

"Well, I guess I'll go on to work tomorrow," I commented to my wife.

"I thought you were going deer hunting tomorrow," she answered with disbelief. "You have been planning the hunt all week."

However, with 30 years of deer hunting experience I know that the worst weather conditions for trying to bag a buck are wintertime bluebird days. Deer are not as active on these types of days as other days. A hunter is less likely to see a nice buck on a bluebird day than at any other time of the season.

When the sun is not as high and the weather is not as nice, I believe deer, especially older, more mature bucks, use shadows and shade as cover and camouflage. We know the first deer to respond to hunting pressure are older bucks. Often they will be the first deer in the herd to become nocturnal when hunting pressure is high.

On Cold Days

"The next three days may be the coldest days of the year," the weatherman reported. "The temperatures will be down around zero."

There are two schools of thought about hunting during severe cold weather. The first school teaches that because the weather is so cold, few hunters will be out in the woods. Therefore, hunting pressure will be lighter, and the deer will be moving about more. The other school of deer hunting takes the position that deer respond to severe cold weather by seeking shelter and holing up until the temperature warms up.

Dr. Larry Marchinton thinks that during severe cold weather deer seem to move less than they do during more stable conditions.

"I don't have scientific research to back this theory," Dr. Marchinton comments. "However, I do know from my own experience I see fewer deer moving on extremely cold days than I do when the weather is stable."

During Stable Weather

"I believe that after a cold front has passed through and the weather becomes stable, the deer are very active," Dr. Marchinton continues. "True -- deer do move ahead of a front. However, I feel that two or three days must pass after a severe cold front before deer begin their normal feeding and moving patterns. When bow hunting, I prefer to hunt funnel areas during the rut three or four days after a front to maximize my chances of taking a deer."

The effects of sudden and dramatic weather changes may take longer for deer to acclimate to than we once have thought. For that reason, stable weather conditions may favor the hunter more than any other condition -- except the approach of a front.

Tony Zappia from New York hunts in the snow most of the year and took these two fine bucks on Anticosti Island in one day.

In The Snow

Being from Alabama, I don't have much opportunity to hunt deer in the snow. However, we often will have two or three days of snow each deer season. Having a white blanket covering the ground makes for some unusual deer hunting.

"I had the strangest thing happen to me," well-known big game hunter and outdoor writer, Jim Zumbo of Cody, Wyoming, said.

Zumbo was hunting in Alabama with me on one of the coldest days in the state's history. There was a snow the night before we planned to hunt. We had taken stands over greenfields.

According to Zumbo, "I spotted a nice eight point on the edge of the woods beside the field. The deer approached the field very cautiously. Then suddenly he ran into the opening. The shot was long, but I prepared to make it. However, before I could mount the gun, the deer started darting back and forth. The buck apparently didn't know how to react to the snow. Finally he ran out of the field before I could get a shot. I feel sure the snow was a new environment that the deer didn't know how to react to."

I have found Zumbo's observation to be accurate. When deer see little or no snow, they become very skittish, nervous and wary. Although whitetails are easier to see because of the white blanket covering the ground, so is the hunter. Usually the deer I try to hunt in the snow spot me before I see them. In areas where snow covers the ground during most of deer season, I'm sure this may not be true.

In The Rain

As the weatherman told his viewing audience, "You can expect light, scattered showers tomorrow, and the skies will be overcast," I said to myself, "Tomorrow will be a good day to deer hunt."

Rain has various effects on deer. A light rain doesn't seem to affect their movement patterns at all. But a heavy rain does tend to force the animals into cover. The rain also prevents most hunters from searching for deer; therefore, there is less hunting pressure.

I like hunting for deer on rainy days for several reasons. If I am stalk hunting, the rain hides much of my movement and washes away my scent. Therefore, I often hunt the same area more than once. Determining which way the wind is blowing is easy because of the way the rain is blowing. I also have found that deer don't smell as well in the rain as they do during dry conditions, so they are less likely to wind me. The sound of the rain and the wet ground also muffles my stalk. I can move in closer to a deer without being detected.

Many of us fail to take the deer we hunt, because we overlook details that are major factors in a good hunt plan. One of those factors is the weather. Once you begin to study and try to predict the weather's effect on the deer and the hunters, you soon will realize that listening to the weatherman the night before you hunt and the morning before you hunt will influence the way you hunt, the place you hunt and whether or not you hunt. To consistently stay abreast of weather conditions, purchase a portable weather radio. Weather affects all of us -- even the deer we hunt.

CHAPTER 10

WHY NUTS ARE THE BEST BET
FOR BUCKS

AS THE SUN cast daggers of crystal white light through the trees to illuminate the forest floor, Craig Hawkins sat in his treestand in hopes of seeing a buck.

Hawkins recalled later that, "There was a scrape line just on the edge of the lip of a ridge that overlooked a hardwood bottom. The acorns had been falling in the bottom for several days. The rut was about to begin. I assumed this active scrape line would be a fine place to bag a buck since not only was there a place for a buck to meet his does but also food close by."

As more slivers of light announced the coming of a new day, Hawkins spotted a glint of ivory at the end of the trail. In the early morning light, he could see a buck coming up the trail on the edge of the ridge.

"I also watched a doe moving down in the bottom feeding on the acorns at the same time," Hawkins explained. "I noticed the buck kept an eye on the doe and moved parallel to her, although he didn't drop off the ridge to feed on the acorns or meet the doe. He continued to come toward me."

As the buck drew closer to Hawkins, Hawkins mounted his rifle and prepared for the shot. Finally when the buck stepped into a small opening, Hawkins' crosshairs found the point of the buck's shoulder, the trigger was squeezed, and the trophy went down.

"Most hunters try to hunt too close to a food source like acorns rather than hunting well away from that food source so as not to spook the deer they are trying to take," Hawkins said. "If I only can hunt one type of area to attempt to bag an antlered buck any day of the week, I'll hunt nuts."

Your best bet for bagging bucks in most woodlots will be around nuts. But unlike most nut hunters, Hawkins does not believe the best time to hunt nuts is when the first acorns start to fall.

"During the first two days when nuts fall, I have learned you may have a difficult time finding deer around nut trees," Hawkins reported. "When an abundance of nuts is on the ground, deer will come in, fill up quickly on nuts and be gone. But when fewer acorns are available, the deer must search for them more intently. They will remain under the same trees longer and will move from tree to tree much more frequently than when they can eat their fill of the nuts they want under a single tree."

Hawkins, who is one of the owners of Hawkins Ridge Lodge near Eufaula in deer-rich East Alabama, each fall goes into the woods to study the acorn crop, learn deer movement patterns and determine where the most productive places are to locate treestands.

"Some years certain nut trees won't bear nuts," Hawkins observed. "Also some trees will bear nuts with a blight on them, such as pecans sometimes have. Even if the tree does bear, you must test the nuts to learn whether or not they are good, if the meat of the nut is small, and whether or not they have worms in them. Don't assume the acorns on the ground are what the bucks are looking for just because you find an acorn tree producing acorns."

Hawkins suggests cracking the nuts to learn if the shells are full of meat and if the meat looks fully mature with either a rich white or yellow color to it.

"Deer search for the best nuts they can locate, not just any nuts," Hawkins mentioned. "This is one reason you often see deer feeding around one tree more than another tree that produces the same type of nut -- even in the same area. One tree may be getting more and better nutrition and producing sweeter-tasting nuts than the other trees. The tree yielding the better nut is the tree the deer will target for feeding."

Hunt The Bucks Up, Not Down

Often a hunter will sit in a hardwood bottom where the nuts are abundant on the ground and wait for a buck to move into the bottom to feed -- trying to take the buck while sitting on top of the deer's

One of Craig Hawkins' most productive areas are the ridges above the acorns.

dinner table -- but not Hawkins. When Hawkins hunts nuts, rather than being in a bottom, he prefers to take a stand on the lip of a ridge overlooking a bottom.

"Deer usually will go into a bottom from a ridge rather than walking through a bottom, especially if that acorn flat is dry and full of leaves," Hawkins said.

Hawkins believes deer know they make noise when they move through a bottom like this but make less noise when they move along a ridge and then drop off into the bottom. "Hunters also spook numbers of deer with their noise when they are walking through these acorn flats," Hawkins commented.

By moving along the lip of a ridge, Hawkins has learned he not only can move quieter than if he walks through the bottom, but he often can see more. Hawkins stalks off the top of the ridge to keep from being silhouetted against the sky. Also deer are less likely to see him if he is above them rather than on the same plane with them. Too, if he is down in a bottom, he cannot view as much property as he can if he is on the lip of the ridge. Another reason Hawkins chooses to hunt the ridges above acorns is because in the morning when he likes to hunt over acorns, air currents known as thermals cause the upward movement of air, which can eliminate his human odor that can and will spook deer.

"In the mornings, a general up-current of air occurs because the air is cooler than the earth below it," Hawkins explained. "Therefore, the air rises. If you are in the bottom of an acorn flat, your scent will rise on either side of the two ridges making up the bottom and will alert deer on both ridges. However, if you're on the top of the ridge, that upward current of air will carry your human odor up and away from your hunting site."

Know Your Nuts

Where Hawkins hunts in the South, the red oaks, water oaks and pin oaks begin to drop their nuts first. Usually the deer will concentrate under these types of oak trees. During bow season and the first part of gun season, even when there are croplands nearby, deer still will feed on acorns as well as agricultural crops. But, when the larger white oaks begin to drop their acorns, the deer's feeding patterns will change radically.

"We have some corn food plots on our land that deer will hit hard during the first of the season," Hawkins reported. "But as soon as the white oak trees start to drop their acorns, the deer will leave the cornfields to feed on the white oaks."

In Hawkins' section of the United States, deer usually will target white oak trees for feeding more specifically than they will red oaks, water oaks or pin oaks. The variety of oak trees Hawkins hunts over determines his strategy and where and how he will set up to take a shot at the deer.

"Generally one or two white oaks will be in an area," Hawkins said. "When the nuts begin to fall, the deer will feed under these specific trees. Therefore I'll hunt around the individual tree on which the deer are feeding. If I am hunting white oak trees, I'll take a stand just at the outer range of my shooting distance to the particular tree I will be hunting. Then I won't spook deer as they come in to feed.

"But when hunting in a region with numbers of water oaks, red oaks and/or pin oaks, I hunt the trails going through the feeding area rather then the individual trees. The deer will meander through this region --making well- defined trails. Particularly if I am hunting red oak trees, which tend to group together in stands, I have found the

Bucks particularly enjoy white oak tree nuts.

most productive way to hunt is to hunt the trails or bottlenecks where the red oak trees form small funnels through big woodlots."

But if you are bow hunting, try and place your stand within 20 to 30 yards of the nut-producing tree, regardless of the type of nut tree. When gun hunting an area where you can make a 50 to 100 yard shot, try and take a stand that will put you at least that far away from the tree.

"Many hunters get too close to the nut trees," Hawkins advised. "Deer will feed under these trees all day long. If a young buck or a doe comes in to feed and sees or smells you, he or she may spook a bigger deer behind them. The further you take a stand away from the tree, the more deer you probably will see in a day of hunting."

Double And Triple Dip Nut Trees

According to Hawkins, deer will feed under the same nut trees at three different times of the year. Hawkins has observed that when a tree first drops its nuts, the deer will concentrate under that tree. But they often will leave that tree or group of trees when nuts are more abundant under another tree. This first dropping of the nuts represents the first time the deer feed under these trees.

The second time the deer will come to these same trees is after all the trees have dropped their nuts. Then the animals return to feed on many of the same trees they have fed under when that particular tree first has dropped its nuts. They also will have to look harder to find more nuts. During this second feeding cycle, the deer

93

do not concentrate on one particular tree as they do when that tree first drops its nuts. But they will return to many of the trees they have fed under during the first of the season to try and find additional nuts later in the season. Rarely will deer find all the nuts under a tree during the first or second feeding cycle.

Then later on in the year if heavy rains pour into a woodlot, the acorns that are left under those same trees will float to the surface, wash into low spots and puddles and concentrate like caches of gold nuggets in a pocket of a stream. After the water subsides, the deer will search for these small pockets of acorns and feed heavily on them.

"If an area has a flood, the acorns will float to the surface and wash into eddy holes," Hawkins explained. "The deer actually will move out into the water and feed on the acorns there. During high water if you can find a line of acorns along the edge of flooded timber, you'll often see deer moving along this line and feeding on the acorns on the edge of the water."

Nuts Are A Reliable Hunt Site

Deer do not read magazine articles or solunar tables. They move and feed whenever they want to and not only early in the morning and in the late afternoon. During the rut, bucks will feed all during the day. When hunting pressure is high, they may eat in the middle of the day. When you are hunting under a nut tree, you can expect to see a buck at any time of the day. Nuts are the natural browse whitetails feed on whenever available.

Honey Hole Nut Trees

According to Hawkins, certain nut trees hold secrets to bagging bucks.

"When most hunters see an oak tree standing alone in the middle of a clearcut, they won't bother to go to that lone nut tree and try and hunt near it, and why should they? Plenty of areas have numerous nut trees. But what they often fail to realize is an isolated oak tree that is producing nuts in a clearcut will provide a food source for deer in thick cover where they are protected and may concentrate deer in that one spot better than a large group of nut trees will in a woodlot with other nut trees."

Hawkins also searches for acorn trees in pine plantations.

"Oftentimes a red oak or a white oak tree will stand on the edge of a firebreak, along a gully or a ditch or in a turn-around spot in the

Look for acorn trees in thick cover corridors. Deer often return to the same tree year after year.

middle of a pine plantation," Hawkins mentioned. "This nut tree will provide food in thick cover areas and can and will concentrate bucks."

Another honey hole nut tree may be an acorn tree surrounded by a briar thicket or a tree on the edge of a patch of cane near a river or a creek bank.

"Any place where you find a producing acorn tree close to thick cover, you often will find a deer feeding site," Hawkins reported. "Mature bucks like to remain in thick cover during hunting season. If they only have to move a yard or two out of that thick cover to feed, then they may hit those acorn trees on the edge of thick cover during daylight hours. If during hunting season, the acorn trees are out in open woods the bucks still will feed on them. However, most of the time they will eat on these nuts after dark."

If you plan to hunt big bucks around acorns, look for thick cover corridors the bucks can use to reach these trees without exposing themselves in the open woods. These acorn trees may provide the best opportunity for you to bag a buck this season.

CHAPTER 11

HUNTING DEER ON TRAILS

IN ONE AFTERNOON on my first bow hunt and my first experience at using a sight on a bow, I drew on and shot at 24 different deer, although I never cut a hair. Because I'd only read about pinsights, never actually had seen one and didn't know where to buy one, I created my own using a finishing nail with a spot of white house paint on the head and a heavy-duty rubberband. I moved the nail up and down on the bow until I consistently could hit a bull's-eye target at 30 yards I had set up in my backyard.

However, when I climbed a tree on my first hunt, the nail on the front of my bow must have moved slightly. After I'd missed the first three deer, I tried to adjust the nail so I could shoot accurately. But the homemade pinsight never worked well -- even though I had plenty of targets.

Several telltale signs indicated I had set up my treestand along a deer highway. A small, narrow trail led from the acorn flat where I had taken a stand over a bank into a clearcut that had grown up in briars and brambles so thick that walking through it was impossible. The small trail the deer were utilizing between their feeding and bedding areas presented a clean, 20 yard view of deer coming and going. Although the animals could have crossed this bank at any point, for some reason this particular spot was the location they all chose to move back and forth on between their bedding and feeding regions. Surprisingly enough, no one else who hunted this land had found this whitetail interstate. Although I failed to arrow a buck, I had some of the best shooting I'd ever had as an archer.

Whitetail Highways

Several different kinds of paths or trails are used by deer. Some are obvious, and many are inconspicuous. If you know what to look for and where to look, you can take a stand and drastically increase your ability to find and bag deer. Mike Fine' of Spirit Lake, Iowa, a member of the advisory hunting staff for Oneida Bow Company, often detects the movement of deer on all types of trails with fishing line.

"Sometimes I string one pound or two pound monofilament fishing line high enough across a trail that a raccoon or a dog normally won't trip it, but a deer will. However, whether that line is broken or not, I take that line out of the woods with me when I leave, because monofilament stays in the environment for some time. I check every trail I hunt to see if deer are using it."

Meandering trails are routes without clearly defined paths deer travel from one point to another. Most hunters won't be able to find these routes easily. Another kind of trail is a terrain trail, which deer utilize frequently that is well-defined to traverse mountainous terrain, converging terrains or some other type of geographic structure that makes walking easier for the animals.

Hidden trails that are invisible to the hunter are used by bucks during certain times and under specific weather conditions. Once you discover these trails, you may have the opportunity to bag more and/or bigger bucks that you've ever taken. Also mating trails and water trails are productive places to find bucks.

Although food trails often are easiest for most of us to find, many don't know how to harvest deer along these trails once hunting pressure begins to build. Also bedding trails can be reliable places to hunt if you know how to find them and when and where to hunt them. Escape trails are routes deer use to flee from hunting pressure. Night trails are what most of us locate and hunt over, yet they produce the least number of deer.

Let's determine how to find various kinds of trails and how to hunt them.

Meandering Trails

Sometimes deer take routes through the woods without leaving trails. Even when deer frequent a particular area, they may not walk

Mating trails are where bucks often will move to find and pick up does.

down a certain path as they move through this region but instead will meander through the woods.

Often meandering trails are present where two types of habitat pinch down a woodlot and create a funnel. Most of the time, deer will meander through that funnel rather than taking a specific route. For instance, if a field or a clearcut corners nears the bend of a creek, there may be only 30 to 50 yards of woods between the creek and the field where the deer prefer to walk, although there may be a large expanse of woods on either side of this small neck of woods. If the leaves are falling or already on the ground in this region, little if any sign may be on the ground for you to see. Even though this route is a deer highway, it may not be easily distinguishable.

According to Sam Spencer, Assistant Director of Alabama's Game and Fish Division and a longtime deer hunter, "Hunting a funnel that narrows down to one specific area improves the odds of the deer coming by you, instead of their walking past you out of range. For example, where a dead tree is down in a funnel area that deer must walk around is a good place to set up your stand. Any break in the funnel where deer must pause to go under a fence or to cross a stream also will be productive spots for taking deer, because the deer are stopping and thinking about how to traverse the obstacle rather than thinking of danger. Too, they're not spending as much time looking up in the trees if they're negotiating an obstacle in the funnel."

Mike Fine' emphasizes the importance of being well-concealed when hunting along any type of trail. "Regardless of what people say, deer are becoming accustomed to humans hunting in trees, and they're looking up in those trees. I like to have my treestand in a cluster of trees if possible, to add concealment. Besides always placing my stand on the downwind side of a trail, I generally wear one of six different camo patterns, depending on the terrain and the time of the year. In a treestand where the leaves are gone and you'll be close to a tree, Trebark camo is hard to beat. A new camo is Skyline camo, which has a light background so you blend in with the sky. Early in the year, obviously a green leaf pattern may be best. In autumn, I go with a brown camo to blend with the changing leaves."

Terrain Trails

Because terrain trails concentrate deer coming and going from two different directions onto a very narrow path, they can be highly productive for the bowhunter. A terrain trail often will be in the saddle between two mountains, because this saddle is the lowest place to cross the mountain range. By taking a stand on either side of the mountain, the hunter has the best chance to take a buck.

If you place your stand in the middle of a saddle and spook deer, the animals may run back the way they've come and spook other deer that are coming up the trail. However, if you take a stand on either side of a saddle, if a buck does spook, he either may run to the

By hunting trails to bedding areas, you often can get close enough to bag a buck with black powder.

left or right instead of back up the trail from where he has come. Then you'll have an opportunity to shoot at deer coming down the trail all day long -- even if your spook one or two animals.

Another type of terrain break deer often will utilize in flatlands is to walk a creek bottom or a wash through thick cover. As Clarence

Yates, owner of Yates Archery in Birmingham, Alabama, who has taken more than 100 deer with his bow, mentions, "Deer like the path of least resistance just like humans do. A small creek crossing that is grown up on each side and has an opening in the brush will be where deer usually will go through that opening -- just like people will."

One of the easiest types of terrain trails to find is a path along the edge of a creek or a riverbank. Traveling along the edges of water gives deer an instant and immediate terrain break they can use to put between danger and themselves. If hunters or other predators spook the deer, the animals quickly and easily can jump into the river or cross the creek and utilize water as a barrier to protect them from their pursuers.

Depending on how the creek or pond is situated where you find such a trail, the best method of hunting it may be to either wade the water and hunt from the water and/or if possible, put up a treestand on the opposite side of the creek from the trail, if the creek is small. Or, if the pond is a backwoods pond with flooded timber, place your treestand in one of the trees out in the pond. Then you can approach and leave your stand by wading the water and eliminate the human odor you normally will leave on the ground.

Mating Trails

During the rut, deer often will walk mating trails. As a buck expands his territory to try and service more does, he often will have a regular route he travels in search of females. He's much like the 16 year old boy who has a new, shiny car and knows where the girls hang out. He swings by the video shop, the fast food joint and the mall before making one or two more stops looking for girls before he returns home every Saturday night.

Water Trails

The swamp had flooded, and acorns were floating on the surface of the knee-deep water. From the numbers of cracked acorns on the bank, I knew deer were feeding in this site, although I couldn't find any tracks. I decided to sit on the edge of the slough all day to see where the deer were moving and feeding.

In the early morning light, I could hear acorns popping and water pouring as I made out a dark figure in the two foot deep water. Using my binoculars, I focused on the object and saw a fat doe knee-deep in the flooded timber picking up acorns in her mouth, letting

Trophy deer stay on the most remote trails, often harder to reach by most hunters. A small four-wheel vehicle is sometimes helpful.

the water run out of her mouth, cracking the acorns and eating the meat of the nuts. In 2-1/2-hours, I watched 15 other does moving along the edges or in the shallow water eating acorns. These deer were walking an underwater path that led through the flooded timber and their food.

Once on another flood plain, I located deer tracks going into the water just at dark. The next morning I set up a treestand 20 yards from where I had seen the tracks going into the backwoods beaver pond. As I watched, deer moved back and forth across the pond -- apparently on an underwater ridge that was only four or five inches below the surface but yet was not visible from the shore. Hunting this underwater ridge produced two fine bucks for me during that season. Each year since when floodwaters have filled the backwoods, I've bagged a deer there.

Food Trails

Food trails are the easiest and most obvious places for hunters to attempt to take deer. However, where you set up on a food trail is vitally important to your success. An easy food trail to follow is one that leads to an agricultural field, because generally the deer will enter the field at a corner, a point or some other obvious passageway. Take a stand 20 or 30 yards inside the woodline along the trail that goes to the field. However, the more often the trail is hunted, the more sensitive deer become to hunting pressure, and the more likely they are to stay well down the trail before dark.

As Sam Spencer comments, "I set up well away from a food plot to intercept a deer earlier, since many deer won't enter a foodplot until almost dark to be safe. Then the light's too bad for me to shoot accurately."

Often the bigger, better-sized bucks will wait just before dark 100 to 200 yards down the trails that lead to the greenfield. If you can find an alternative food source like an acorn tree or some wild vegetation deer are feeding on along that trail leading to the greenfield, you've located an excellent spot to bag a buck. I've watched bucks come down a trail leading to a greenfield, stop under an acorn tree and begin to feed waiting on nightfall.

The deer remind me of party-goers who nibble on hors d'oeuvres before the banquet feast is served. By taking a stand near that snack food, you may have the opportunity to bag the big buck no one ever sees on the greenfield.

One of the best areas to take deer is at a particular tree where deer are feeding. The most productive food trees are the isolated ones. For instance, if you find one apple tree in 500 acres of hardwoods where deer are feeding or one white oak acorn tree, which is the deer's preferred food in my area of the country, the deer in that region probably are coming to that tree to eat. Because several trails from various directions lead into that food tree, you may not be certain where to place your treestand. However, you can funnel deer from one trail to another by using human odor as a barrier on the trails you don't want the deer to travel down.

Ronnie Groom, a deer hunting instructor at numerous schools across the South, suggests that, "Move 150 to 200 yards away from the food tree, and walk across each one of the trails you don't want the deer to use -- being careful to leave plenty of human odor on these trails. When the deer come down the trail you've tried to X out, they will smell human odor, leave the trail they're on, and move to the trail you want them to walk down that doesn't have human odor on it."

Bedding Trails

Hunting the buck as he goes to his bed presents another hunting opportunity. In most areas when deer are being pressured, they will move to their beds just at daylight. By locating a buck's food source and where he beds, you can place your stand and climb in it before daylight.

Mike Fine' emphasizes that, "I get as close to a bedding area as I can without disturbing the deer so I have the most light. I hunt farther off the trails than most people I know and always on the downwind side. I think one of the mistakes people make is hunting too close to where they anticipate the shot."

In scouting a bedding region, you should spend as little time as possible to determine where to put your treestand because as Fine' observes, "Deer won't feel secure in a bedding area if they detect human odor. Always scout bedding sites in advance of deer season before the bucks become so sensitive to human sightings and smell. Also I don't cross any bedding trails if I can avoid them and will go out of my way to not cross them."

Clarence Yates reports that, "You never should hunt a deer's bedding area when the wind's blowing in the wrong direction. If you're hunting next to lowlands, remember air usually will move from higher elevations to the lower part of a hollow in the evenings. So set up on the lower side of the trail going to and from where the deer's bedding. If you plan to hunt a bedding trail in the morning, don't forget that because air rises at that time, you should place your treestand on the upper side of the trail.

"If I can't get to a bedding site well before daylight and be on my stand that's set up with a favorable wind direction, then I hunt another place that day. I've learned if I spook a buck coming to his bed, more than likely that's the last time I'll see that animal during the season."

Escape Trails

Apartment buildings, hotels and department stores all have fire escapes. Even elevators have trapdoors in their ceilings. Then, in case of emergency, people have a way to escape danger.

The whitetail realizes the presence of danger in his environment, especially during hunting season. That's why the buck has certain pre-determined paths he uses to escape danger. Often these trails will not be well-defined and may show little wear. But they are the routes through the wilderness bucks especially will utilize to dodge hunters.

One of the most unusual escape trails I ever discovered was under a bridge. Each morning before hunting season when I was scouting, I noticed a nice buck in a greenfield on a club I hunted. However, when the season arrived, I rarely saw the buck in the field but would spot him on the opposite side of the creek at first light as I went into the woods to hunt.

After scouting for several weeks, I still couldn't pinpoint how the buck was getting away from the field to the opposite side of the creek. Finally one morning, I left to hunt somewhat earlier, and the buck apparently was a little late leaving the greenfield. I watched as he walked under the bridge I traveled across to go hunting. When daylight came, I found the buck's trail where it went into the water just below the field. Checking under the bridge, I saw a small sandbar with plenty of tracks going both ways the buck was using to travel back and forth to the field. I told a friend of mine about this escape route, and the following morning, he took the buck.

As hunting pressure builds, and deer become more aware of the hunter's presence in the woods, finding these escape trails, often in heavy cover or in unusual places, can be highly productive.

Night Trails

I'm totally convinced many of us waste thousands of hours hunting over trails deer never use during daylight hours. One of the best ways to decide whether or not a trail you're looking at is a night trail is if it has numbers of tracks on it and goes straight in one direction. These are the trails deer use to get from point A to point B. The animals don't meander along these trails and feed, walk these trails in search of does or take these paths to and from food sources during daylight hours.

Like us when we're traveling from one point to another, deer will take a woods interstate, which is the most direct route. However, if we want to pick up a date, get something to eat or be social with friends, we must get off the highway and so must deer. These night trails are easy to see in open woodlots and appear to be productive

Bucks don't expect to find hunters along thickets and escape trails.

places to hunt. But to pinpoint whether or not these paths are nighttime trails, use a trail timer.

Because these night trails are easy to locate and well- defined, many people will hunt here, although usually the trails will have the most hunting pressure during daylight hours. To avoid the hunter, the deer using this trail only will come out after dark.

Jamie Bulger, an avid bowhunter from Georgia, reports that, "I never bowhunt heavily used trails but instead get off those trails and locate a secondary trail that's downwind of the major trail. Too, I always wear a cover-up scent, usually one with pine odor since I hunt mainly in pine forests, and hang some scent cover-ups around my treestand.

Probably the least productive trail is one in a very open area. When you easily can distinguish a trail going through an open region, and you think, 'Boy, deer are tearing up this place most of the time,' that trail probably is being used during the night because it is so open."

Also as Mike Fine' comments, "Manmade trails in the woods like horse trails, hiking trails, snowmobile trails, etc. are the least productive to hunt -- even though they may have numbers of deer tracks on them. Those trails probably are being utilized by deer only at night. I'm convinced large, mature bucks will not use the heavier traveled trails during the day that most of the immature bucks, does, and fawns travel but rather will utilize trails that are less discernible, usually not far from major trails."

To be consistently effective at taking whitetails, you must find various types of trails and learn where the deer are going and why they're traveling to these regions as well as when. After gathering that information, try and put a treestand where you can bag a buck. When a big buck moves down that deer highway at a time you have pre-determined he will, and you sight in on your target, you'll understand immediately why all your research and scouting for trails has been worthwhile.

CHAPTER 12

THE TRUTH ABOUT THE RUT

WHEN WHITETAIL BUCKS or those who hunt these deer lose their minds and become totally obsessed with sex, both species become very vulnerable. Luckily for the deer, this insanity only occurs once a year. Because bucks in the rut chase does, that's when the animals are easy to bag. Hunting during the rut offers the best opportunity to take a trophy. But what triggers the rut? What's the truth about the rut? To learn the answers to these questions, we talked with some of the leading wildlife scientists of our day: Dr. Keith Causey, professor of wildlife science at Auburn University in Auburn, Alabama; Charles DeYoung, professor at Texas A & I in Kingsville, Texas; Horace Gore, wildlife biologist at Texas Parks and Wildlife in Austin, Texas; Joe Hamilton, assistant regional wildlife biologist at South Carolina Game and Fish in Columbia, South Carolina; Harry Jacobson, professor in the Department of Wildlife & Fisheries at Mississippi State University; and Bob Zaiglin, wildlife manager for Harrison Interests, Ltd. in Uvalde, Texas.

What Triggers The Breeding Season

JACOBSON: The doe actually triggers the breeding season for the buck. She defines the rut when she is in estrus. Dr. Larry Marchinton at the University of Georgia in Athens, Georgia, has broken the rut down into three periods: pre-rut, rut and post-rut. Some fighting takes place during the pre-rut, when a buck claims his territory by leaving signposts like rubs and scrapes. The rut itself

109

begins when the first doe comes in estrus with the peak of the rut occurring some three weeks after the first doe is in estrus. If does are not bred during their first estrous cycle, they can have a second or a third cycle in a season. Also a peak of the rut may happen during the post-rut, because first-year does usually will come into estrus later, around two or three months after the older does. Therefore bucks often will be chasing does much longer than we hunters expect.

DE YOUNG: The answer of what triggers the breeding season for the buck is complex. The general season is controlled by the light cycle -- the lengthening and shortening of daylight hours. Another factor is nutrition. If deer are in excellent physical condition, then generally the breeding season or the rut will be a little earlier. Temperature also has an effect on deer breeding. If the time for the breeding season to begin is close, a sharp, cold spell will stimulate sexual activity and set the deer off.

GORE: A buck is probably in a breeding condition for quite awhile before the does begin to come into heat. A buck's system probably gets ready to breed around mid-September, because he has all the capabilities of breeding the doe as soon as his testosterone level builds up to the point where he's polishing his antlers.

ZAIGLIN: Some of our deer in South Texas start breeding in early December with older does and continue all the way into May, because the fawns that are just starting their first cycle have received enough nutrition from the spring rains to be able to breed.

When The Rut Begins

ZAIGLIN: The changes in the amount of daylight from the summer to the fall increases the amount of testosterone in the animal. That increased testosterone level steps up the calcification process of the antlers. As the length of daylight hours shorten, antlers solidify, and the rise in testosterone facilitates breeding in the bucks.

DE YOUNG: The buck starts exhibiting rutting behavior such as fighting, scraping and rubbing. Behavioral scientists are debating whether or not this male activity perhaps in some way stimulates the female's estrous cycle. However, no one has proven this idea.

HAMILTON: As the rut begins, the bucks become more solitary, whereas before they have been more fraternal and traveled together. Bucks start making rubs with their antlers and leave

110

signposts with different kinds of pheromones, which are chemical substances produced by deer that serve as a stimulus to other deer for behavioral responses. Deer have pheromones in their saliva, in their forehead region and near their eyes in glands, which enlarge only during the breeding season. A buck not only rubs his antlers but also his forehead and his eyes on bushes and limbs besides crunching limbs with his mouth to leave his scent. 80 percent of the time, an overhanging branch will be above where a buck makes a scrape. The buck reaches this branch with his eyes, mouth and forehead to leave more scent. Also bucks urinate on their hind legs, which have glands that secrete certain scents. The fluid from these glands mingles with the urine that drips down the buck's hind legs to act as a signpost.

Doe Behavior

CAUSEY: Decreasing photo periods (the amount of daylight) trigger the onset of the estrous cycle in does during the fall and winter, while the photo period change during the spring seems to turn the does off so they don't breed.

HAMILTON: Many hunters are misled. Actually does actively are looking for bucks just as diligently as bucks are searching for does during the rut. The decreasing daylight levels that trigger the testosterone levels in the bucks also are making the breeding juices flow in the does.

ZAIGLIN: If a doe has a high nutrition level, she can come into heat on an early schedule. However, if she has built up too much fat, this can inhibit her estrous cycle. A doe that has had twins may come into estrus later, because she's been drawn down nutritionally the year before.

How And When Ruts Occur

JACOBSON: The time of year the rut occurs varies according to geographic locations. Not only is there a photo period relationship to the rut but also a genetic relationship. The rut may occur as early as mid-August in certain sections of Florida, and some very northern herds may do some September breeding. Generally, the rut in the North occurs from mid- October to November. As you get farther South, the breeding season may come in as late as January and February in certain places.

HAMILTON: When talking about breeding seasons, a huge variation exists -- even in neighborhoods -- because of various

111

management techniques. Where I live in South Carolina, today the breeding season peaks about the first week of October, because the existing bucks are more alike in antler development than ever before. For the last five years, we've taken precautions in our state to insure four does for every buck. So we've shot out bucks very selectively, according to size. To be bagged, the bucks must have a 15 inch spread. However, six years ago when South Carolina had many does and few restrictions on the bucks taken, the state had breedings of whitetails taking place for more than six months out of the year, depending on locality. Today a graph of the breeding of whitetail deer in South Carolina shows a very sharp, definite peak in October rather than what a graph once illustrated when the breeding of deer resembled the teeth of a saw blade.

CAUSEY: The rut lasts from October to April or May, depending on where you are. In certain parts of the country, the breeding season is spread out all over the winter; in other regions, the rut is very precisely defined and occurs primarily within a 30 day period. In Alabama and other parts of the Southeast, the breeding activity occurs over a three or a four month period.

DE YOUNG: Also the rut varies some according to the sex ratio -- the number of bucks to does. If many more females are included in a herd than are males, the breeding season may last longer, because the males can't get around to service all the females while they're in heat. Often the females will cycle again. Generally, if you're in the northern part of the whitetail deer's range, the breeding time is short. But the length of the breeding time usually increases as you travel South, since the rut is tied to the photo period. In South Texas, the rut lasts about three months. Deer found in South America and close to the equator may experience an even longer rut.

How The Rut Affects A Buck's Home Range

CAUSEY: Well, if a buck leaves an area, then the region is not his home territory. The home range is the land he covers during his lifetime. He may leave his most frequented area and go on excursions, which will expand his home range to include more territory.

GORE: As the does in the buck's home territory are bred, a dominant buck that's high-up in the pecking order will start searching more widely for another doe in heat and will cover a lot of territory. In the latter part of the breeding cycle, the older, more dominant bucks tend to cover more ground searching for a doe in heat.

112

Bucks in the rut chase does to breed.

JACOBSON: Generally, the scientific evidence shows the doe goes in search of the buck -- not the other way around. Once she finds him, he may follow her out of his territory. If the buck is outside his normal home range, probably he's consorting with an estrous doe that has come into his territory and has lured him out.

ZAIGLIN: During the rut, bucks are active up to 24 hours a day but don't necessarily move outside their range. More often than not, these bucks will have more does on their home ranges than they're capable of breeding. A buck is polygamous and may breed 100 does or more a year. But only so many does are going to be in estrus at one time. In Pennsylvania for example, which has eight to 11 does per buck, rarely does a buck have to move around much to locate does to breed.

Why Subordinate Bucks Breed Does

CAUSEY: Yes, other bucks breed the does because the dominant buck can't be looking after all the estrous females at the same time.

113

GORE: In Texas, we have so many does coming into heat and so few dominant bucks, that if enough does come into heat at the same time, the pecking order on which animal gets to do the breeding may include some subordinates. Not that many dominant bucks are in a region, and often 2-1/2-year old bucks are numerous. So they do some breeding too.

JACOBSON: In most deerherds, the exploitation pressure on the males is so heavy that fewer older bucks are around. Often the bulk of the breeding is being done by 1-1/2-year old deer that don't have much of a dominant hierarchy established. Even in deerherds with mature males, sometimes the older bucks get preoccupied with one another. The younger ones may sneak in while the mature bucks are concentrating on their rivals and trying to hold their positions in the herd, particularly if the rivals are closely matched. Usually the mature, dominant male will do the bulk of the breeding. Also some older bucks may not be that interested in breeding, because their sexual libidos are not as strong as some of the younger bucks that have become more active and visible during the rut.

ZAIGLIN: Even in a tight sex ratio with equal numbers of bucks and does in a herd, always some bucks will be more aggressive than others. Obviously, the younger bucks will attempt to do some breeding, if they can. These young, healthy bucks are more aggressive because they're trying to reach a position in the breeding community. Breeding does is like a status symbol. These deer may not be big-antlered. Even spiked bucks may breed. Which buck breeds a doe depends on when a doe comes into heat, where she's in heat, and how many other does are in heat at the same time. If the ratio of does to bucks is skewed very heavily in favor of the female segment, then a buck will breed as many as he can. However, some does will be available for other bucks too.

How Bucks Fight During The Rut

ZAIGLIN: Although very few small bucks try to fight older bucks, sometimes they do. Older bucks have more of a tendency to fight other mature bucks and are more likely to really hurt each other. Older bucks spend much time exercising a lot of aggression, which makes them very stressed during the breeding period and reduces their energy.

CAUSEY: Bucks fight during the rut by sparring or play fighting. Once their antlers are polished, they establish a dominance

114

By knowing when the rut occurs in your state, you will understand when your odds are best for bagging a buck like this.

hierarchy through vigorous fighting or bluffing displays. However, any time controversy arises between two males about which is dominant, a serious fight usually will be the result. Most of the time though, this aggression is satisfied either by posturing or bluffing rather than actual physical fighting.

GORE: Deer do a lot of fighting. Usually the older they are, the more they fight. The younger a buck is, the less fighting he will do. When bucks are about three years old, one buck dominates another buck quickly, without actually fighting but rather by sparring. But the very aggressive, older bucks may hurt each other over the breeding.

Why Bucks Pick A Fight

CAUSEY: If a buck fails to yield to the dominant buck with proper posturing and proper behavior, the dominant buck will fight the buck that's new to the area.

ZAIGLIN: No set boundaries exist on acres. Often deer's boundaries overlap, and many bucks may pass through an area. What bucks don't do is share their breeding periods. In the summertime, bucks normally will travel together. They're a highly compatible species until breeding begins.

GORE: A dominant buck and a new buck in a region probably will fight only if there's a doe in heat. If the bucks are just roaming around looking, they won't fight. But if both are covering a wider territory than usual and one has a doe in heat with him, and he's trying to keep her away from other deer, then there's liable to be one big fight.

DE YOUNG: There's some debate about whether biologists ought to even say deer are territorial, because to a scientist, the word, territory doesn't simply mean the area where deer roam. A deer's territory also means he defends the region from other deer.

How Weather Affects The Rut

ZAIGLIN: The weather absolutely is a critical factor. In South Texas, we may have 95 degree days, even in December. When the weather's dry and hot in December, sexual activity will be suppressed, but the deer don't quit breeding. Deer breed regardless of the temperature, although they may do it more lethargically or nocturnally and not necessarily in the daytime. Weather may play a role in what we see of the rut, however, it doesn't necessarily stop the rut.

CAUSEY: Yes, cooler weather allows more vigorous activity of the deer without creating heat stress. When cool snaps occur during the time of year when rutting takes place, the weather encourages a lot of chasing, playing, running and other types of activities people associate with the rut. So cooler weather can bring out the more aggressive activity.

GORE: I don't think weather has anything to do with the rut other than deer obviously are more active on a cool wind from the North than they are on a hot, southern wind. Although you may see

Bucks often avoid fights by exhibiting aggressive postures during the rut.

more activity in cool weather, the deer probably are breeding even when the weather's hot.

JACOBSON: Weather may have some effect on delaying or moving up breeding dates. Weather definitely plays a role in buck activity and is a factor in a buck's energy level. If the day is hot and humid, a buck's not going to feel as much like fighting as he will if the weather is brisk and cool. Just like us, if things are nice outdoors, we feel good; if the weather's muggy, we aren't in the mood for doing much. So I think there are some behavioral indications, mainly in terms of a buck's aggressiveness toward other deer that the weather dictates. But in terms of whether or not the doe's going to breed, weather matters very little.

CHAPTER 13

HUNTING THE RUT

WILDLIFE SCIENTISTS and deer hunters have amassed a wealth of knowledge about scrapes, the rut and hunting tactics during the breeding season, which usually is the best time of year to take a trophy buck. However any time a large amount of information is gathered, there often also is myth blended with fact. To learn how to hunt the rut successfully, we must understand how and when it occurs and the sequence of events that's involved.

Prior to breeding, bucks go through a cycle where they establish their dominance. Bucks, which are traveling in buck groups and can't care less about does at that time, begin to spar as soon as the velvet is rubbed off their antlers. This time is when rattling antlers may be an effective technique to lure in bucks. You even may call in more than one buck at a time.

Then four to six weeks after the deer start to spar, which is very different from bucks fighting, the buck groups break up. Mature bucks begin to chase does -- perhaps because of an increased level of male hormone production, a change in the scent of the doe as she approaches estrus and/or a combination of the two factors. When this occurs, taking a stand in areas where you have seen does all season may be your most productive tactic.

When bucks chase does they trail behind them at a distance of about 150 feet or more, since usually the doe will not allow the buck to approach any closer before she goes into estrus. Scientists have discovered that after a buck has chased a doe about the length of five football fields, he may give up the chase. However at the very beginning of the rut, before the does have come into estrus strong, the buck may run after the doe for a shorter distance before quitting.

Also remember that more than one buck may pursue a doe at the same time, because all breeding age bucks participate in the courtship chases. But usually the larger bucks are the ones closest behind the does. The smaller bucks will be following behind the dominant buck. Even a doe may be in line behind a younger buck. Therefore, if you spot a doe running through the woods during the rut, look for a dominant buck behind her. If you do not get a shot at him, do not give up, because there may be a smaller buck coming along the same path in a few minutes.

Through years of research, biologists have learned much about deer and the rut. During the rut, a buck loses much of his natural wariness and sacrifices caution for the right to breed. He travels more during the day, leaves more tracks in the woods for the hunter and often is easier to pattern than at any other time of the year.

But determining which hunting methods are the most productive to use during the rut is difficult. When you begin to discuss the rut, you immediately begin to talk about scrape hunting, which has been known to be an effective way to take a buck during the rut. To dispel fiction from fact, we asked Dr. Karl V. Miller, a deer researcher who also is an avid, longtime deer hunter, to give us some ideas about how to hunt the rut and to explain the facts about scrapes, scrape hunting and other aspects of the rut.

Scrapes

"I've read in popular articles that there are many types of scrapes including boundary scrapes, primary scrapes, secondary scrapes, mating scrapes and territorial scrapes," Miller recalls. "But I'm not aware of any studies that substantiate that bucks make scrapes for various reasons. Also, I've read at various times that scrapes always are made in a criss-cross pattern, they usually run from East to West, they most always run from West to East, they are made only by dominant bucks and/or only one buck will visit a scrape. However much of the information written about scrapes that hunters talk about is just not true.

"To understand how to hunt the rut, we must learn who makes the scrapes. Although generally the earliest scrapes you see in the woods will be made by the dominant buck, a large percentage of the

Rattling antlers may be a very effective technique to lure in bucks during the early fall.

scrapes in any area will be made by mature bucks that are not necessarily the dominant buck in that region. Remember an area doesn't home only one mature, dominant buck, with all the other bucks in that region timid and suppressed. As long as the mature bucks in an area are not together, then each buck is dominant, because the only time one buck is dominant over another buck is when two mature bucks get together. Then dominance is expressed.

"Mature bucks are like youngsters who want to be bullies. As long as there is no one bigger or tougher than the bully on the block, then he's dominant. But if a bigger, stronger, tougher kid moves on the block, the original bully is no longer the dominant one. Instead there's two big, strong, tough guys in the neighborhood -- each the strongest when the other is not around.

"Also, some bucks are more aggressive about making scrapes than others, which is a tendency that doesn't have anything to do with dominance. Some big bucks just like to make numbers of scrapes, whereas other mature bucks choose not to make any scrapes. Don't ever overlook the fact that each deer is an individual with different traits and characteristics, which is part of the reason that coming up with an absolute hunting tactic that always works for taking bucks during the rut is almost impossible."

Miller feels that what is most important is determining which scrape is used the most by the buck.

"Bucks frequent some scrapes more often that they do other scrapes. I think a mature buck may be much like a single man in his prime who goes to several different bars to meet women. The bar where he is the most successful is the one he will frequent most often. Sometimes deer will follow this same pattern. The scrapes where bucks most often run into does perhaps will be the scrapes they come to the most."

"Scientists aren't sure that a scrape's primary purpose is to attract does. We do know that the scrape is a signpost bucks use to communicate to other bucks and does that there's a mature buck in the area. But subordinate bucks as well as dominant bucks will come to a scrape and leave their scents on the overhanging branch above the pawed earth. Very rarely, however, will you see a subordinate buck urinate in the scrape, because this right usually is reserved for the maker of the scrape."

This information may solve one of the riddles of hunting the rut. Many have wondered why they have bagged small, young bucks at scrapes which usually are made by mature bucks. To take a trophy buck instead of just any buck, allow the young bucks to pass when they come to a scrape, and wait for the mature buck to show up later.

"I believe when a dominant buck comes to a scrape he leaves the scent from his mouth, eyes, nose and forehead on the overhanging branch to say, 'I'm here,'" Miller explains. "By pawing in the scrape, he may be demonstrating some aggression. Perhaps by urinating in the scrape he leaves some kind of indication of his physiological makeup and how big and strong he is. I think what he's telling the subordinate bucks is, 'I'm dominant, and I'm willing to fight if you mess with me or my does.' I also believe that when the subordinate

Learning which scrape to hunt can help you take trophy bucks during the rut.

buck walks up and puts his scent on the overhanging branch, he's leaving a message for the dominant buck that says, 'Hey, I'm in the area, and I'm no threat to you.'"

"If a doe in estrus can't find a dominant buck to breed her, then perhaps she goes to a scrape because she understands that the scrape is made by a mature buck and that he checks the scrape from time to time. She probably realizes that if she's there when he's checking the scrape she may be bred by one of the better bucks in the region. This is nature's way of insuring survival of the fittest."

Therefore, you may have the option while hunting a scrape during the rut of bagging either a mature buck that supervises a scrape, a subordinate buck that is just at the scrape to say hello, or a doe that comes into to the scrape looking for a buck to breed her. Just because you see a deer at a scrape doesn't mean you can assume you're watching the deer that has made the scrape, because that nice-sized buck at the scrape still may not be the biggest buck around that actually has made the scrape. When you locate an active scrape and decide to hunt that scrape, let the other deer pass by the scrape unharmed, if you're only hunting a trophy buck.

Rubs

Besides making scrapes, bucks rub trees during the rut, often around scrapes and along trails to scrapes. Most of us tend to think that little bucks rub small trees and big bucks rub large trees.

But according to Miller, "Although probably little bucks rub mostly little trees, I know big bucks rub both small and large trees. When a deer makes a rub, he wants to leave a visual key and a scent key on a tree for other deer to see and smell. From what I've seen and learned in the woods, whether the buck leaves that message on a big tree or a little tree is not important. At times I've watched big bucks rub tiny trees, but usually they don't. If the bucks are very big, they'll overpower the tree they rub."

If you are hunting a buck during the rut, your chances of seeing that buck may be just as likely on a trail with a series of rubs that leads to a scraping area as your chances are while hunting directly over a scrape. Yet another advantage to hunting rubs leading to a scrape is that often the wind may be blowing from the wrong direction for you to hunt that scrape. However, if the trail with the rubs on it turns in a direction that allows you to hunt that trail with a favorable wind, you may bag a buck and definitely will be more effective than if you hunt the scrape with the wrong wind.

A Perennial Hotspot

Many of us believe if we take a buck at a scrape there is a very good chance that the next year there may be a mature buck using that same scraping site, which should mean that you can take a buck at this spot year after year.

Miller mentions that, "The scrape where a mature buck is harvested may be a good place to hunt the same year, because scrapes generally are made in travel corridors and areas where deer frequent. However, evidence doesn't support that deer remember making a scrape on any certain tree. But scientists have learned that deer will mark the overhanging branches over a scrape throughout the year. These same overhanging branches that the deer are marking may turn into scrapes during the rut.

"These overhanging branches have been written up in popular literature as licking sticks. Although I can't say that the licking stick

Travel corridors can help you find that elusive buck.

deer use to communicate with each other all year long becomes a scrape during the rutting season, however, I do think this is a good guess and can happen."

Mock Scrapes

Hundreds of articles have been written on the value of hunters making mock scrapes to try and fool a buck into believing that another buck has invaded his territory.

"Although I believe the mock scrape concept can work, I don't know that I will go to all the trouble required to make a mock scrape to try and take a mature buck," Miller observes. "Rather than just pouring buck urine in the ground that you've torn up under an overhanging branch, remember the key to making a mock scrape is to locate an overhanging branch that is at the correct height and in the right place and then make the mock scrape. I'm convinced the deer scent left on the branch is more critical to getting a buck to come in than the urine poured into the mock scrape.

"Personally I've found that instead of making a mock scrape and hoping to fool a buck, the hunter who spends his time finding a hot scrape a buck is already working to hunt over will be more successful in probably less time. I believe hunting over the real thing is better than hunting over an imitation of the real thing."

Active Scrapes

If you find a scrape with a strong urine smell, you assume that the buck has worked this scrape recently. Some believe that if they take a stand near this scrape they will get a shot at a dominant buck.

But Miller comments that, "Bucks don't always go back to scrapes once they've made them. However, scrape hunting is a deadly tactic during the rut, because there is a possibility the buck may return. But there are no guarantees. I've learned there are very few absolutes about deer movement and/or behavior. Also in areas of high hunting pressure, a buck may work his scrapes at night."

Productive Scrapes

Miller advises that, "The best scrapes to hunt over are the scrapes found in travel corridors, because these regions will be where the deer naturally funnel through to move from one place to another. Scrapes in a travel corridor greatly increases your chances of observing deer."

In heavily hunted areas, the rut often provides the best opportunity for you to take a mature buck.

However as Miller notes, "Deer, especially mature bucks, are individuals with their own idiosyncrasies and their own methods of dodging hunters, breeding, making scrapes and chasing does. Until you are willing to recognize the mature buck as an individual, learn his peculiarities and spend the time in the woods to get to know his haunts, then you won't be able to consistently harvest mature bucks.

"Although the rut is the easiest time of the year to take a mature buck, you must understand that any time of the year you bag an older age buck, you either have to outsmart that deer by knowing more about what he is going to do and when he is going to do it than he does or just get lucky."

CHAPTER 14

FACTS & MYTHS ABOUT ANTLERS

WHAT CAN YOU learn about deer from antlers? Do bucks grow new antlers each year? If a buck is an eight point deer one year, will he be a nine point the next year? What causes some deer to have high, wide-racked antlers, while other deer may have narrow, spindly antlers?

These are just a few of the questions we posed to two of the nation's leading wildlife scientists -- Dale Sheffer, the Director of the Bureau of Wildlife Management for the state of Pennsylvania, and Dr. James G. Teer, Director of the Welder Wildlife Foundation in Texas.

Of fascination to all of us is the fact that deer shed their antlers each year. According to Dr. Teer, "A pedicel on each of the frontal bones on the deer's skull supports the antlers. After the breeding season, a reduction of testosterone and other hormones in the deer causes the base of the antlers, called the abscission layer, to weaken. Finally, the antlers will fall off like the leaves of a tree. A leaf always breaks away from the branch at the stem, which is the same way antlers break away from the abscission layer on the skull. I've seen antlers fall off when a deer merely shakes his head."

Dale Sheffer compared a deer's antlers growing and then being shed each year to a cancerous growth.

"Antlers are much like a cancerous growth as the antlers grow very fast and have a large blood supply sent to them during the time of year the antlers grow. But once the antlers fully mature, the blood supply is turned off to the antlers, which makes the antlers hard. As the amount of light per day declines, the blood recedes from the antlers causing the antlers to die. The antlers become like a scab or a sore and then either drop off or fall off one day."

Deer experience no pain when their antlers drop off, because no feeling is present in the antlers, which have no blood supply. If a buck's antlers are removed prior to the breeding season, more than likely he won't breed.

Sheffer mentions, "If that buck is the only male in the herd, he will breed. But even a little spike buck will breed does if the herd buck loses his antlers before breeding season. The antlers do contribute to the buck's ability to breed a doe."

By studying shed antlers after the season, you can look at an array of antlers picked up over a number of years and see trends in antler development.

As Teer emphasizes, "For instance, if you picked up as many shed antlers as you could find on a particular piece of property, perhaps during one year, and the total weight of those antlers was five kilograms, and then the next year you gathered antlers of all age classes on that property, and the antlers weighed six or eight kilograms, you'd know the antlers on this specific place were larger. But also some age biases would exist."

Nutrition Is The Key

When asked about what can be determined from the number of points on a deer's rack as well as its size, Dr. Teer replies that, "No direct correlation exists between the number of points a buck has on its rack and the age of the animal. However, generally, younger deer will have smaller antlers than the older deer. Once bucks are adults, their antler development depends more on the amount of nutrition they receive than any other factors. The amount of food, the quality of that food and the general well-being of the individual deer are some of the major contributing factors to antler growth and development.

"Although a theory at one time has been that a spike always will be a spike, this concept is not valid. However, some evidence does show that spikes can be controlled genetically. Spikes may produce smaller antlered bucks later in life than fork-horned deer do. But I believe 90 percent of the influence on antler development is dependent on the nutrition of that animal."

When the deer is in the velvet, his antlers grow because of the blood supply going to them.

Sheffer comments that studies done in Pennsylvania have revealed that if a buck gets all the food he needs until he is 5-1/2-years old, his antlers usually will grow bigger each year. But at the age of 6-1/2-years, a deer's antlers often begin to decline and actually may be smaller than they have been earlier in a buck's life. However, a 1-1/2-year old buck on a high protein diet can be an eight point.

Teer also reiterates the importance of nutrition on a deer's antler development by pointing out that a big, healthy 10 point buck in Texas will have much smaller antlers the next year following a spring and summer of drought.

"That 10 point deer only might be an eight point during the next hunting season. A buck we observed at the Welder Wildlife Foundation for three years had progressively larger antlers until the third year when he experienced a drought and a reduction of food. Then his antlers were smaller."

Although the diameter of the base of the main beam one inch from the base of the antlers is a measurement biologists commonly take when studying antler development, some hunters think this diameter measurement of the main beam relates to a deer's age. But both Teer and Sheffer caution that the diameter of the main beam generally provides more information about the nutrition level and the general health of the animal than it does age.

"Mostly bucks that are older will have antlers with a larger diameter base than younger bucks," Sheffer reports. "However, if a buck goes through a severe winter with little available food and loses a large amount of body weight, then he won't put on antlers as large as he has had the year before, even though the base of the antlers, the pedicel, will remain the same size or grow slightly. Because a buck's body's number one priority is to keep the animal alive, only left-over nutrition will be used to build antlers."

Age And Genetic Factors

Other contributing factors in the size and weight of antlers are the age and the genetic makeup of the deer. Some hunters claim to be able to determine the age of a buck by the number of points the deer has as well as the length of the points, the spread of the rack and/or the weight of the rack.

Dr. Teer advises that a loose correlation does exist between antler development and age.

"You can tell a deer is young if his rack is not much wider than his ears, and the diameter of the main beam and the diameters of each of the points are about the diameter of a pencil. When that buck stands next to a deer with a wide, high, heavy rack, determining which deer is the older is not difficult. Although hunters may be able to visually note the difference between a young buck and an older buck, I don't believe they can look at a deer and state positively the animal is a three or a four year old."

Sheffer observes that the tendency toward wide racks is a genetic characteristic more than a characteristic of age.

"Genetic studies at Penn State have demonstrated a young buck's antlers will look much like the antlers of the buck that sires him. But another factor in the genetic make-up of a buck's antlers is the general health and physical condition of the mother. A healthy doe is as critical if not more important to big bucks with heavy antlers as a good sire."

The Dominant Buck

Other questions often asked are whether the buck with the largest antlers in the herd is genetically superior, and is he the dominant buck?

"The buck with the biggest antlers in the herd can be the dominant buck but very well may not be the most genetically superior animal in the herd," Teer observes. "A young buck in the herd with smaller antlers may be genetically superior to all the other bucks and possess antlers bigger than what the biggest buck has -- if that young buck is allowed to survive long enough to demonstrate his genetic superiority. Also a young buck, if allowed to mature, may transmit better genes to his offspring than the biggest buck in the herd at any given time.

Some hunters may think they should harvest the younger bucks they consider not on par genetically with the older deer to clean up the gene pool of the herd and make it stronger. But those younger bucks may have better genes than the older ones. You can't visually pick out a genetically superior buck from a group."

Sheffer reminds us that, "A dominant buck always is the strongest and toughest buck in the herd -- no matter what his antlers look like. A dominant buck may be like a 143 pound tough guy who is as strong as a 200 pound muscle man. If the animal with smaller antlers is a stronger and better fighter than the buck with bigger antlers, then the younger, stronger deer will be dominant. Although often the heavier antlered buck will have a decided advantage over a buck with smaller antlers, this is not always true.

"Also remember that not just one dominant buck may live in an area. For instance, if four bucks and 40 does are in a two square mile region, one buck can't breed all 40 does -- no matter what his antler size or what position he holds in the herd."

Unusual Racks

The various racks deer can sport such as palmated, drop-tined, malformed and non-typical often have been the subject of discussion wherever hunters gather. When I asked Sheffer what causes a buck to have a palmated rack, he answered that, "Because this genetic trait is passed from one sire buck to its progeny, not all deer have palmated racks. In certain sections of particular states, you'll see this palmated characteristic in individual deer herds.

"For many years, hunters in Pennsylvania wanted the Bureau of Wildlife Management to import deer from Michigan, because the Michigan deer seemed to have more palmated antlers. However, we talked to the wildlife scientists in Michigan, who felt that the palmation of antlers wasn't a general characteristic of their entire herd but rather occurred in isolated herds. The palmation of antlers of deer families often is like the hair color of people with the same genetic characteristic."

Teer comments that a non-typical rack can have several causes, including influences through genetics.

"Sometimes an injury to the antler will cause it to be atypical. For instance, a dropped-tine, which often is sought out by hunters, can be a genetic trait in a particular deer herd. High basket antlers and a wide rack also can be genetic traits."

Sheffer explains that numerous factors can cause a malformed rack. "Oftentimes when the deer are in velvet, the antlers are almost the consistency of jelly sitting on top of the animal's head. Even a small piece of brush hitting the antlers can injure them and cause them to grow in an unusual form. Or, the antlers may be snapped off while the antlers are soft.

"In early to mid-April when the antlers first start to appear, the antlers contain a large blood supply, which makes them very vulnerable to insects like the blow fly. If the blow fly lays its eggs in the deer's soft antlers, the eggs will form cups or depressions in the antlers. If an intensive case of insect infestation occurs while antlers are in the velvet, the result will be deformed looking antlers. Antlers also may be broken off during the rutting season when deer fight, and a testicle injury can cause the buck's antlers to be malformed."

Effects Of Overpopulation

Another major concern of sportsmen is the effect of overpopulation on antler development.

"Overpopulation will mean a decrease of the deer's food supply, because too many deer for the land to support means all the deer are on short rations," Teer says. "Overpopulation will result in less antler development and smaller bodied bucks."

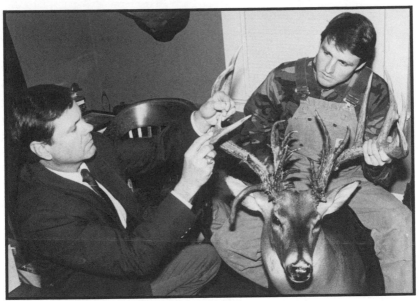

Drop-tines like these often are a genetic characteristic.

Sheffer mentioned that generally more deformed antlers will be present in an overpopulated deer herd since competition for food is so great.

"Some parts of Pennsylvania have more than 200 deer per square mile. When this occurs, unless supplemental feeding is practiced, the herd will have stunted deer with smaller quality racks because they do not get enough nutrition by the time they're weaned to put on heavy racks. In some sections, 2-1/2- and 3-1/2-year old bucks only may have 3-1/2-inch spikes.

"If the herd size is reduced, then the more food the deer on specific lands have, the larger the deer will grow, and the heavier the buck's antlers will be. That's why big deer come from states like Maine where you only may see one deer during a week of hunting, but that deer may be a large buck with heavy antlers."

Teer suggests the most effective way to produce more bucks with heavy antlers is to make sure the habitat is right for producing big bucks with trophy racks, including plenty of food, particularly in the winter.

"Also be certain you harvest a sufficient number of animals to keep the deer herd in balance, since most landowners and sportsmen don't. When the carrying capacity of the land reaches a point where competition exists for food among the deer and also between the deer and the domestic livestock, antler development and body weights will go down. Too, that food must be within easy access of the deer. The more nutritious food a deer has to eat, the better antlers he will put on."

Yet another major controversy is whether or not supplemental feeding of deer will increase antler size. As Sheffer states, "Some people think supplemental feedings will increase antler size of deer. Biologists know this is true of deer in captivity. But if you're feeding deer in the wild, supplemental feeding can be terribly expensive, since the supplemental food also can be eaten by other animals such as raccoons and porcupines. However, planting food crops is a cheaper, more effective way of feeding deer than pouring food out on the ground and hoping the deer will eat it.

"Alfalfa and ladino clover are excellent crops you can plant for deer. In my part of the country, alfalfa is one of the best foods for deer. When possible, the hunter needs to increase the amount of nutrition in the food the deer has to eat."

According to Teer, a better approach to deer management than putting out food supplements is to manage the deer's home range the way it is.

"For instance, there are regions in South Texas that are deficient in phosphorous. To be sure the deer get this mineral, you can add phosphorous to the deer's water supply or in blocks to the deer's feed. However, not many scientific studies have proved this management tool is appropriate for increasing the general health of deer.

"I believe planting food crops -- cereal grains like winter oats, wheat and rye as well as clover -- during certain seasons of the year when the habitat is in its worse conditions can increase the nutritional level of deer. At this time of year, the deer already are in hard antler. But by improving their body conditions during the winter months, then when spring arrives, the deer will be in much better shape for growing larger antlers than they will have been than if they have come through the winter in poor condition."

Although hunters search for large, high, wide, heavy antlers, I'm amazed at how little I actually know about how antlers grow and develop and what factors must be present to produce trophy racks in deer.

CHAPTER 15

TRUTH AND FICTION ABOUT DEER TRACKS

THE FIRST TIME someone told me he had seen a big buck's track on a dirt road headed into a thicket, I wondered how he knew the difference between a buck's track and a doe's track. I was both amazed and mystified at his vast knowledge of whitetails.

Through the years in any hunting camp I've been in, always a track expert has been in residence who can tell the size, sex, and age of a deer by its tracks. I've stalked deer before that the width of their tracks have convinced me they were bucks. Also I've had hunters tell me that seeing the dew claws as part of the deer's track is a definite indication the animal that has made the track is a buck. Because so much misinformation exists about deer tracks and what information they can communicate to those of us who hunt, I have talked to wildlife biologists and avid deer hunters to learn the truth about deer tracks.

Telling The Sex

"The only sure way to know if a deer track you've found is that of a buck or a doe is to see that animal standing in its track," Dr. Bob Sheppard says.

Although most wildlife scientists agree with Sheppard, Bob Zaiglin, wildlife biologist and manager for several Texas ranches, explains that, "Knowing the lay of the land is more important to bagging a buck than seeing deer tracks. But some experienced hunters can distinguish a buck by the size of the track and more

Can you look at this track and tell whether it is a buck or a doe?

importantly by the spread of the feet. A buck's dew claws hang down somewhat, and sometimes a buck will drag his feet and turn a little more dirt up when he walks than a doe does.

"In South Texas, where most of our company's ranches are, knowledgeable veterans can tell a buck from a doe because the bucks tear up more ground than the does. However, the average neophyte will have a very difficult time judging the sex of a deer just by the footprints."

Joe Hamilton, assistant regional wildlife biologist for South Carolina Game and Fish, believes most hunters think they can determine the sex of the deer by the size of the deer's track, which Hamilton will not say is totally impossible. However, Hamilton believes that, "In much of the East, 90 percent of the bucks being harvested are only 1-1/2- year old animals. When the hunter spots a big track on the ground, more than likely he's looking at the track of a large doe, since in many areas the does are allowed to live longer than bucks, become bigger as they get older and make a larger track. However, in regions with snow, sand and/or mud, the buck may drag his feet and/or make deeper tracks."

Harry Jacobson, professor in the Department of Wildlife and Fisheries at Mississippi State University states that sometimes you can and sometimes you can't tell the tracks of a buck from a doe. "If the tracks are very large, then a good chance exists that the tracks may have been made by a buck. But generally speaking, determining the sex of deer from tracks is very difficult."

Ronnie Groom comments that, "The medium the track is in and the speed at which the deer is moving often determine the size of the track more than the weight and the size of the animal do. If a 100 pound doe jumps off a small hill onto a muddy road, she may leave a very wide, big track with dew claws showing. But if a 250 pound buck walks up a hard clay, creek bottom, he may not leave a very wide track because the ground doesn't give way and absorb the weight of his body, which will leave a bigger track. I personally try not to determine the sex of a deer by its track."

I'm convinced anyone who hunts needs to gather much more information to be successful afield rather than trying to determine the sex of the deer by any of the physical characteristics or the size of a track.

Track Size

All the biologists and hunters we asked this question of gave much the same answer. The size of the doe's tracks often will be determined by the management program being conducted on the lands where you're hunting. In much of the East, more does that are older are in the deerherds than those in states like Texas, which have been managing deer intensively for numbers of years.

According to Jacobson, sometimes deer populations are so badly managed that hunting pressure eliminates a large majority of the bucks, whereas the does are treated like the sacred cows of India, allowed to put on heavier body weights and reach much older age classes than the bucks do.

"That's why often a doe's track will be bigger than a buck's track in areas where the deerherd contains does that are older than bucks."

Weight And Physical Condition

Although some hunters believe they can tell the size of a deer's rack, the age of the deer, the weight of the deer and other physical characteristics from the animal's track, Charles DeYoung mentions that you can note some general characteristics about deer if you see their tracks side by side, particularly if one track is a fawn's and the other a buck's, but, "Generally you can't determine this, unless you're an Apache."

A well-trained scientific eye like that of Joe Hamilton may be able to detect some physical characteristics from the animal's track that the average hunter may not be able to see.

"You can determine if a deer has a broken leg or not, because the track of the broken leg will be smeared and will make a different impression than the other three tracks of the same animal," Hamilton observes. "However, determining that a deer is light because of parasites or disease is very difficult. If the deer is feverish and taking very short steps, we may be able to determine his poor physical condition, particularly if the animal is walking in a good tracking medium like soft earth or mud. If the deer is very cold and walking stoop-shouldered, he may be taking smaller, shorter, choppier steps, which you also may be able to detect."

Hamilton can make this type of evaluation about a deer's track because he's a scientist who has spent many years studying deer and the tracks they leave. However, the average hunter will be hard-pressed to make these types of judgment calls from the tracks he sees in the woods.

Speed

We asked deer researchers if you can tell from a deer's tracks whether the animal is running or walking. If the deer you're tracking is running, probably you or something else may have spooked the animal, which is alerted and may be very difficult to stalk. But if the

A trail with tracks going in two directions may lead you to a good spot to take a buck.

tracks reveal the deer is walking, a good chance exists that the deer hasn't been alarmed and may be easy to stalk.

Dr. Keith Causey says, "Usually you can tell whether a deer is walking or running by the distance between the tracks as well as whether the toes are spread on the impact from running. If a deer is wounded, obviously one of the legs will be impaired tremendously, and the animal will put much less weight on that leg than on the other. The wounded foot will leave a lighter track."

Dew Claw

Horace Gore says the dew claw does not necessarily indicate a buck made the track. "Often the size of the animal and the medium the track is being placed in will determine the depth of the print and whether or not a dew claw is apparent in the print. In soft mud or clay, even the track of yearling deer may reveal a dew claw. In a freshly plowed field, the print of a dew claw can be present as part of the track. However, a very large buck walking across rock or hard clay may not leave a big track at all or a dew claw print in the track."

Deer Hotspots

Dr. Bob Sheppard has learned that finding a trail with tracks going in both directions often signals he's at a deer hotspot. "One of the best places to find this kind of trail is in a funnel area where the terrain is necked down by two different types of converging habitats. Deer will move back and forth along this trail all day long to get from one section of woods to the other part of woods. Before when I've set up my treestand near a trail with tracks going in both directions, I've seen deer all day long. To me, a trail with two directional tracks is one of the best places for a hunter to take a stand."

Bob Zaiglin emphasizes how important locating trails that meet or intersect is to seeing more deer. "You can look at deer trails in two ways. If the trail goes in two directions, you don't know where the deer are moving to--right or left. But also you may think that several deer are in the region, and they're all coming to this point. For instance, in certain geographical areas, trails come from all different directions with a pivot point where they cross. Where trails cross generally is a productive place to concentrate your hunting."

As Horace Gore mentions, "Obviously if you find a trail with tracks going in two directions, the deer probably are going to a food supply and coming back to a bedding ground. If the tracks only are going one way, then you don't know necessarily what the deer are doing. However, if the tracks are moving in two directions, then you possibly can intercept those deer because they're coming and going rather than just going. If a deer moves out in a forage area tonight and returns to the bedding ground in the daytime, a good time to be along this trail is just at daylight when the deer are coming back."

Planning A Hunt

I've known some hunters who have sat in the same treestand for three or four days because they've found some deer tracks in a spot and are sure a buck will pass by eventually. I'm also acquainted with others who have followed deer tracks over 10-miles of countryside trying to catch up to the deer that have made those tracks. Still

A buck like this may make a large track on soft ground. Walking across hard ground, he may leave a small track.

others I know completely have disregarded tracks and prefer instead to hunt over agricultural fields, at nut trees where the deer feed or in thickets where the animals may bed. So how important are tracks to your hunting plan?

"Obviously, you want to see some deer tracks to reassure yourself psychologically there are deer around," Bob Zaiglin mentions. "But on many places with dry, rocky terrain, like southern Texas and Mexico, you won't see any tracks, even though plenty of deer may be in an area. A medium like rock or dry ground won't hold the impression of the deer's hoofprint.

"As a wildlife manager as well as an avid deer hunter, I don't like to see too many tracks, because that indicates too many deer are on the land. Too many deer mean the animals lack quality and few, if any, will be trophy bucks. The fewer deer in a deerherd, the more likely the deer are to be healthy, older and bigger bucks."

Horace Gore believes tracks can be very important to a deer hunter's scouting successfully. "Seeing deer tracks when you're scouting out a hunting area reminds me of the old saying, 'If a deer is there, he's making tracks.' If you're scouting a spot looking for trails and deer sign but don't find any tracks, probably no deer are in the region."

141

Individual Tracks

Like you, I've known hunters who've said, "I saw the track of ole Mossy Horns down by the creek last Thursday. I'm sure that's him, because I've examined his track for the last three years. He's got a very big track. One of these days I'm going to find him standing in it."

However, Horace Gore is skeptical about a hunter's ability to determine that one particular track has been made by the same deer year after year. "If the deer's track is exceptionally big, you may be able to say year after year that the same deer has made the track. But the deer will have to be an unusually large deer.

"In Texas, deer tracks don't mean that much in helping to denote one deer from another, because the ground is so dry and hard in most parts that rarely will a hunter be able to discriminate the track of one particular deer from another. You may have a better chance of distinguishing a specific deer's track from another in places like Mississippi, Alabama, and/or East Texas, where much of the ground is soft. Still the deer must have an unusual track -- perhaps crippled in some way or a somewhat different-looking foot -- to be discernible.

"In 30 years, I don't believe I've heard anybody in Texas talk about seeing the track of a deer and recognizing it as a deer they've been hunting. In this state, you hear more people talk about identifying deer by their dropped antlers."

Importance Of Tracks

From our experts, we've learned that deer tracks can be important. Bob Zaiglin says that seeing the deer that made the track is far more important than looking at a track and attempting to determine anything about the animal. The main function tracks perform is to notify you that a deer has walked through this place at some time in the past. Discovering deer tracks is no guarantee the same deer will walk back through that region again.

Generally deer tracks do not tell you the sex or the size of the deer. Many of the old wives' tales we've always heard about deer tracks are only suppositions and good conversation fodder for campfire talk.

CHAPTER 16

TRACKING AND TRAILING DEER

YOUR SUCCESS AS a deer hunter does not solely depend on your ability to find a buck, aim precisely and shoot accurately. All your preparation and training will be for nothing if you hit the animal and then cannot recover him.

Although most of us like to believe that the animal will fall instantly when we squeeze the trigger, the truth of the matter is that most of the time the deer will run several hundred yards or further before he piles up. After the shot is fired, the deer has vanished, and a hush falls over the woods, a sportsman is left alone with his thoughts and his ability to trail, track and apply good woodsmanship to find his deer. Of course experience, knowledge and having spent thousands of hours in the woods often will lead you to a deer when all else fails.

A hunting buddy of mine, Jim Brownlee of Birmingham, Alabama, had been hunting the same trophy buck all season. In Brownlee's home state, bow season had begun on October 15. Both gun and bow seasons were to go out on January 31. Every weekend of the season Brownlee was in his favorite tree waiting on his trophy buck to appear. He saw the deer four times but never had the animal within gun range.

During the last week of the season, Brownlee saw a flash of ivory 60 yards from his treestand. A 60 yard shot with a 12-gauge is an extremely long shot. However, Brownlee decided if he did not shoot then his chances of taking his trophy would vanish for yet another season.

"I fired, saw the deer flinch and take off running," Brownlee recalled later. "I was sure I had hit the buck, but I didn't know how well I had hit him. Although I listened to see if I could hear him fall, I heard nothing. After 45- minutes of waiting, I climbed out of my tree and went to the spot where I had fired at the buck."

When Brownlee arrived, he found no blood, no hair and no indication of any kind that his buckshot had gone true.

"But I just knew I had hit the deer," he said.

Because the deer was so big and had run from the area, the track he left in the soft mud was easy to see.

"I followed the track for about a half-mile through the swamp and never saw a drop of blood," Brownlee explained. "Finally I sat down on a log and tried to relive what had happened. Could I really have missed the deer? But when I stood up and started back on the track, I saw one spot of blood."

Then 10 yards from where Brownlee saw the one drop of blood, the big buck jumped up. Brownlee fired three more times. But once again, the buck vanished.

"This time I followed the tracks into a backwater slough," Brownlee continued. "I had heard the deer splash when he went into the slough, but I didn't hear him come out on the other side."

The temperatures that day were in the low teens. Brownlee felt sure his buck was in the water.

"I had been hunting that deer too long and had trailed him too far to let the ice water in that slough keep me from him," Brownlee reported. "I took all my clothes off and waded into the water."

Brownlee was warmed by the thought of finding the trophy buck.

"As fast as the deer was running when he left my sight, I knew he would have to swim straight across the pond rather than turning to the right or the left of it. I thought that if I went straight in the direction the deer went in that my foot should find him."

When Brownlee was in waist-deep, he spotted a patch of white 10 yards in front of him just under the surface of the water.

"At first, I thought the white might be the deer's ear. But when I got closer, armpit-deep, I saw it was the deer's tail."

Grabbing hold of the tail and pulling with all his strength, Brownlee sprinted from the icy depths to his warm clothes on shore.

Hunters sometimes have to follow a buck into the water to recover it.

The deer was a trophy eight point that weighed well over 200 pounds.

"That deer took three of us to drag out of the woods," Brownlee reported with a big grin on his face.

Staying with the track and on the trail and continuing long after most hunters would have given up resulted in Brownlee's taking the deer he had dreamed about all his life. Deliberateness of purpose, knowledge of trailing and tracking and trying to think like a deer paid off for Brownlee.

These actions will pay off for you too. Here are some practical tips that will aid you in finding your downed deer.

Reading The Signs

For the most part when outdoorsmen talk about trailing a deer, they generally mean blood trailing. But there are other very important signs that can point you in the direction of your downed quarry.

Most of these signs will be found at the point where the bullet enters the animal or close to that spot. Stomach content, bone, hair and blood all will reveal information critical to recovery of the deer.

Stomach Content: If stomach content is in the area where the deer has been shot, then the bullet may have been placed lower than the shoulder and entered the gut. From this information, the hunter knows the stalk may be a long one and that the more time he can give the animal to lie down before he starts pursuing him, the more likely he is to find the deer.

Hair: The hair on the site also will give indication of where the deer has been hit. Shorter, darker hair is found on the back of the deer. Lighter colored hair and longer hair comes from the sides of the deer. The longest and lightest colored hair will be found along the stomach and the rear of the deer.

Blood: The more information you can gather at the site that will tell you where the bullet has entered the animal, the more likely you are to recover the deer. If the blood is a bright red or a bright red with foam in it, then you can assume that you have a heart shot or a lung shot and that the animal may be close by. If there is a large patch of blood, you may have a good hit and may not have far to walk to recover your deer. But study the ground carefully where you've shot the deer to gain as much information as possible before you start the stalk.

Following The Deer's Trail

Once you leave the place where you've shot the deer and start to trail him look for two things -- tracks and blood on the ground and the sides of trees and bushes.

Tracks: In areas with low deer populations, tracking a wounded deer may prove to be almost as successful a tactic as blood trailing a deer. When the blood runs out and you still have a good track, many times you can recover your animal.

Blood Trail: The easiest and simplest method of finding a deer is to follow a blood trail to the animal. Many times a well-hit deer will spew blood from the wound and leave a crimson path to his destination. Following a blood trail may be simple but can be very complex and sometimes difficult.

Just seeing blood on the ground merely will tell you that the deer was there and that he did in fact drop blood. However, there is much more that can be learned. If you can determine which way the drops

When you squeeze the trigger, listen and watch what the buck does, in the event you need to trail him.

of blood have splattered, then you can tell the direction of flight of the deer.

When the animal is walking or running, the drops of blood will fall to the ground, hit a leaf and smear in the direction of flight. The blood may look like a teardrop with the little end of the drop pointing in the direction the deer was headed. A big smear of blood on the ground may indicate that either the deer has laid down in that spot or has fallen there.

Look at your compass to determine in what direction the deer is traveling.

Sportsmen often overlook some of the most noticeable signs that will help them recover their deer because they constantly are looking down. If the deer is hit anywhere in the side and there is blood coming from the wound, that blood will stick to trees, bushes and limbs as the deer passes by and rubs them. Don't forget to look about waist-high for this sign.

When the blood trail ends, this point is where many hunters lose their deer. The blood trail has stopped, and they haven't recovered their animal. In many cases, the buck will be within 150 yards radius of the spot where the blood has stopped. But where do you look?

Most of the time a fatally wounded deer will head for the thickest cover he can find before he dies. Fallen treetops, briar thickets, cane patches and berry thickets are all excellent places to search for your trophy. Look back at your flagging tape, and try and determine the animal's direction of flight. By using your flagging tape as a pointer, utilize your compass to follow that same line for 150 to 200 yards. Then come back to the last place you have found blood and begin to work a circle from that place out to within 200 yards. Often you will find your deer.

Flagging tape can help you find your hit deer.

The Right Equipment

If the hunter assumes that he will take a deer and that the deer will have to be trailed to be recovered, then he is ahead of 50 percent of the other hunters who go into the woods. Most hunters lack the essential equipment to find their deer. The equipment necessary for making a successful recovery includes a fanny pack, a deer dragger, fluorescent orange flagging tape, a compass and a knife.

The fanny pack is one of the most useful articles of hunting apparel. In the fanny pack, you can store not only your needed equipment but also your lunch, a small bottle of water and many other essentials that make hunting more enjoyable.

The skinner dragger is made up of a piece of cable with a handle on it and a loop that can be fastened to the deer's antlers. This one piece of equipment increases the hunter's leverage when he starts to drag the animal out of the woods and provides a good handhold and a secure strapping to the animal. Most importantly it makes dragging the deer out of the woods easier.

Fluorescent orange flagging tape can be bought at most hardware stores and sporting goods stores and is extremely useful when following a blood trail. Each time the hunter finds blood he can tie a piece of flagging tape on the tree or bush at eye level. Then any time he loses the trail, he always can go back to an easy starting point. By looking at the flagging tape back down the trail he already has walked, the hunter can determine the flight of the deer. The flagging tape also will aid the hunter in finding his way out of the woods with his quarry once it is recovered.

A compass is one device that has been responsible for saving more lives and locating more deer than any other piece of sporting equipment. Once the hunter finds the blood trail, he should look at his compass to determine first of all in which direction the deer is traveling and where he will be heading if the animal stays on that same course. Also by reading the compass, the hunter will know which direction he will have to take to come out of the woods after the animal is found.

I prefer a lockback kind of knife with a blade that folds up easily and can be carried comfortably. By including a knife in your fanny pack, you can eliminate a lot of weight when you find your downed animal by removing the intestines and field dressing the deer. Then the deer can be brought out of the woods more quickly and easier.

INDEX

A

abscission layer   127
acorns   103
active scrapes   126
aerial photograph   22
Charles Alsheimer   50

B

bedding areas   84, 140
bedding trails   105
binoculars   18, 71, 102
blocks   134
blood trail   146
body language   75
boundary scrapes   120
browse   38, 43, 94
Jamie Bulger   107

C

calcification process   110
Mike Cartwright   62, 66, 67
Dr. Keith Causey   46, 54,
      56, 58, 60, 109-117, 139
Lee Christianson   62-68
clearcut   15, 26, 71, 99
crepuscular   38
cutover   42

D

Charles DeYoung   38, 42,
      76, 138, 109-117
decoy deer   28
deer sign   15

dew claws   136
dominance hierarchy   73, 74, 114
dominant buck   36, 65, 74,
      112-116, 120-123, 131
drop-tined   131
drought   43

E

escape trails   105
estrus   15, 76, 109, 119, 123

F

favorable wind   60
feeding patterns   92
fighting,   110
Mike Fine'   98, 105, 108
flight distance   42
Bob Foulkrod   56, 58
funnel   34, 99

G

Horace Gore,   109-117
greenfield   15, 20
Ronnie Groom   37, 40-43,
      104, 137
grunt calls   80

H

habitat   14, 37, 99
hair   146
David Hale   39, 40-42
Joe Hamilton   109-117, 137, 138
Brad Harris   55, 57, 58
Craig Hawkins   89, 94
Dr. Billy Hillestad   13, 78

home range   38, 76, 112
Horace Gore   46, 49,
        52, 139, 140
hunting pressure   19, 28, 31,
        38, 42, 44, 60, 64,
        82, 106

J

Dr. Harry Jacobson   73,
        109-117, 137
Brian Johansen   62, 68

L

Dr. John Lanier   52
Dr. Larry Marchinton
        62, 66, 76, 109
licking sticks   124
light cycle   110
Linda Robbins Leasher   62,
        66, 68
lures   61, 62, 80

M

malformed   131
man-drive   40
maps   22
mast trees   14
mating scrapes   120
meandering trails   99
melatonin   44
Dr. Karl V. Miller   37, 42-44, 120
mineral   134
mock scrapes   125

N

David Nelson   74, 78
night trails   106
nocturnal   39, 42, 56, 57
non-typical   131
nutrition   110, 111, 128

O

odor   54, 104
overpopulation   132

P

palmated   71, 131
patterning   19, 30
pecking order
            (see dominance hierarchy)
pedicel   127, 130
pheromones   111
photo periods   111
pineal gland   44
pituitary gland   44
polygamous   113
post-rut   109
posturing   115, 116
pre-rut   66, 73, 109
preferred foods   30, 34, 43
primary scrapes   120

R

rattling antlers   78, 80
Terry Rohm   74, 76, 78, 79
rub   15, 110, 124
rut   30, 44, 51, 73, 78, 109,
        111-117, 120, 126

S

saddle   35, 100
Eddie Salter   37
Sam Spencer   100, 104
scent   61, 63, 80, 111
scent posts   66
scope   45, 71
scouting   33
scrapes   16, 28, 30, 63, 89, 110,
        120, 122
sex ratio   112, 114
Dale Sheffer,   127-134

Dr. Bob Sheppard   26, 32, 47,
   54-57, 60, 135, 140
shooting lanes   26, 60
signposts   111, 122
Jerry Simmons   49, 52
solunar phases   46, 52
sparring   114, 119
staging area   20
Michael Stickney   75
stomach content   146
subdominant buck   74
subordinate buck   36, 75, 114,
   122
super-dominance   76
supplemental feeding   133

T

tarsal glands   66
Don Taylor   26
Dr. James G. Teer   42, 43, 127-
   134
temperature   37, 38,
   48, 51, 110, 116
terrain trails   100
territorial scrapes   120
testosterone   110, 111, 127
topographical maps   22
tracks   146
trail timer   107
trails   40
travel corridor   20, 126

W

weather   116
Bruce Whitman   62, 64, 66

Y

yarding   40
Clarence Yates   32, 101

Z

Bob Zaiglin   77, 109-117,
   135, 140

FISHING & HUNTING RESOURCE DIRECTORY

If you are interested in more productive fishing and hunting trips, then this info is for you!

Larsen's Outdoor Publishing is the publisher of several quality Outdoor Libraries - all informational-type books that focus on how and where to catch America's most popular sport fish, hunt popular and exciting big game, camp, dive or travel to exotic destinations.

The perfect-bound, soft-cover books include numerous illustrative graphics, line drawings, maps and photographs. The BASS SERIES LIBRARY as well as the HUNTING LIBRARIES are nationwide in scope. The INSHORE SERIES covers coastal areas from Texas to Maryland and foreign waters. The OUTDOOR TRAVEL SERIES and the OUTDOOR ADVENTURE LIBRARY cover the most exciting destinations in the world. The BASS WATERS SERIES focuses on the top lakes and rivers in the nation's most visited largemouth bass fishing state.

All series appeal to outdoorsmen/readers of all skill levels. The unique four-color cover design, interior layout, quality, information content and economical price makes these books hot sellers in the marketplace. Best of all, you can learn to be more successful in your outdoor endeavors!!

THE BASS SERIES LIBRARY
by Larry Larsen

1. FOLLOW THE FORAGE FOR BETTER BASS ANGLING VOL. 1 BASS/PREY RELATIONSHIP
Learn how to determine the dominant forage in a body of water, and you will consistently catch more and larger bass.

2. FOLLOW THE FORAGE FOR BETTER BASS ANGLING VOL. 2 TECHNIQUES
Learn why one lure or bait is more successful than others and how to use each lure under varying conditions.

3. BASS PRO STRATEGIES
Learn from the experience of the pros, how changes in pH, water temperature, color and fluctuations affect bass fishing, and how to adapt to weather and topographical variations.

4. BASS LURES - TRICKS & TECHNIQUES
Learn how to rig or modify your lures and develop specific presentation and retrieve methods to spark or renew the interest of largemouth!

5. SHALLOW WATER BASS
Learn specific productive tactics that you can apply to fishing in marshes, estuaries, reservoirs, lakes, creeks and small ponds. You'll likely triple your results!

6. BASS FISHING FACTS
Learn why and how bass behave during pre- and post-spawn, how they utilize their senses and how they respond to their environment, and you'll increase your bass angling success! This angler's guide to bass lifestyles and behavior is a reference source never before compiled.

7. TROPHY BASS
Take a look at geographical areas and waters that offer better opportunities to catch giant bass, as well as proven methods and tactics for man made/natural waters. "How to" from guides/trophy bass hunters.

8. ANGLER'S GUIDE TO BASS PATTERNS
Catch bass every time out by learning how to develop a productive pattern quickly and effectively. Learn the most effective combination of lures, methods and places for existing bass activity.

9. BASS GUIDE TIPS
Learn the most productive methods of top bass fishing guides in the country and secret techniques known only in a certain region or state that may work in your waters. Special features include shiners, sunfish kites & flies; flippin, pitchin' & dead stickin', rattlin', skippin' & jerk baits; deep, hot and cold waters; fronts, high winds & rain.

INSHORE SERIES
by Frank Sargeant

IL1. THE SNOOK BOOK
"Must" reading for anyone who loves the pursuit of this unique sub-tropic species. Every aspect of how you can find and catch big snook is covered.

IL2. THE REDFISH BOOK
Packed with expertise from the nation's leading redfish anglers and guides, this book covers every aspect of finding and fooling giant reds. You'll learn secret techniques revealed for the first time.

IL3. THE TARPON BOOK
Find and catch the wily "silver king" along the Gulf Coast, north through the mid-Atlantic, and south along Central and South American coastlines. Experts share their most productive techniques.

IL4. THE TROUT BOOK
You'll learn the best seasons, techniques and lures in this comprehensive book. Entertaining, informative reading for both the old salt and rank amateur.

BASS WATERS SERIES
by Larry Larsen

Take the guessing game out of your next bass fishing trip. The most productive bass water are described in this multi-volume series, plus ramp information, seasonal tactics, water characteristics and much more, including numerous maps and drawings and comprehensive index.

BW1. GUIDE TO NORTH FLORIDA BASS WATERS
From Orange Lake north and west.

BW2. GUIDE TO CENTRAL FLORIDA BASS WATERS
From Tampa/Orlando to Palatka.

BW3. GUIDE TO SOUTH FLORIDA BASS WATERS
From I-4 to the Everglades.

DEER HUNTING LIBRARY
by John E. Phillips

DH1. MASTERS' SECRETS OF DEER HUNTING
Increase your deer hunting success significantly by learning from the masters of the sport. New tactics and strategies.

DH2. THE SCIENCE OF DEER HUNTING
Specific ways to study the habits of deer to make your next scouting and hunting trips more successful. Learn the answers to many of the toughest deer hunting problems a sportsman ever encounters.

TURKEY HUNTING LIBRARY
by John E. Phillips

TH1. MASTERS' SECRETS OF TURKEY HUNTING
Masters of the sport have solved some of the most difficult problems you will encounter while hunting wily longbeards with bows, blackpowder guns and shotguns.

OUTDOOR TRAVEL SERIES
by Timothy O'Keefe and Larry Larsen

Candid guides with vital recommendations that can make your next trip much more enjoyable.

OT1. FISH & DIVE THE CARIBBEAN - Volume 1
Northern Caribbean, including Cozumel, Caymans, Bahamas, Virgin Islands and other popular destinations.

OT3. FISH & DIVE FLORIDA & the Keys
Featuring fresh water springs; coral reefs; barrier islands; Gulf Stream/passes; inshore flats/channels and back country estuaries.

OUTDOOR ADVENTURE LIBRARY
by Vin T. Sparano

OA1. HUNTING DANGEROUS GAME
Know how it feels to face game that hunts back. You won't forget these classic tales of hunting adventures for grizzly, buffalo, lion, leopard, elephant, jaguar, wolves, rhinos and more!

158

LARSEN'S OUTDOOR PUBLISHING
CONVENIENT ORDER FORM
ALL PRICES INCLUDE POSTAGE/HANDLING

FRESH WATER

___ BSL3. Bass Pro Strategies ($14.95)
___ BSL4. Bass Lures/Tech. ($14.95)
___ BSL5. Shallow Water Bass ($14.95)
___ BSL6. Bass Fishing Facts ($13.95)
___ BSL8. Bass Patterns ($14.95)
___ BSL9. Bass Guide Tips ($14.95)
___ CF1. Mstrs' Scrts/Crappie Fshg ($12.95)
___ CF2. Crappie Tactics ($12.95)
___ CF3. Mstr's Secrets of Catfishing ($12.95)
___ LB1. Larsen on Bass Tactics ($15.95)
___ PF1. Peacock Bass Explosions! ($16.95)
___ PF2. Peacock Bass & Other Fierce
           Exotics ($17.95)
___ PF3. Peacock Bass Addiction ($18.95)

SALT WATER

___ IL1. The Snook Book   ($14.95)
___ IL2. The Redfish Book ($14.95)
___ IL3. The Tarpon Book ($14.95)
___ IL4. The Trout Book ($14.95)
___ SW1. The Reef Fishing Book ($16.45)
___ SW2. Masters Bk/Snook ($16.45)

REGIONAL

___ FG1. Secret Spots-Tampa Bay/
           Cedar Key   ($15.95)
___ FG2. Secret Spots - SW Florida ($15.95)
___ BW1. Guide/North Fl. Waters ($16.95)
___ BW2. Guide/Cntral Fl.Waters ($15.95)
___ BW3. Guide/South Fl.Waters ($15.95)
___ OT3. Fish/Dive Florida/ Keys ($13.95)

HUNTING

___ DH1. Mstrs' Secrets/ Deer Hunting ($14.95)
___ DH2. Science of Deer Hunting ($14.95)
___ DH3. Mstrs' Secrets/Bowhunting ($12.45)
___ DH4. How to Take Monster Bucks ($13.95)
___ TH1. Mstrs' Secrets/ Turkey Hunting ($14.95)

OTHER OUTDOORS BOOKS

___ DL2. Manatees/Vanishing ($11.45)
___ DL3. Sea Turtles/Watchers' ($11.45)

FREE BROCHURES

___ Peacock Bass Brochure
___ LOP Book Catalog

BIG MULTI-BOOK DISCOUNT!

2-3 books, SAVE 10%

4 or more books, SAVE 20%

INTERNATIONAL AIRMAIL ORDERS

Send check in U.S. funds; add $6 more for 1 book; $4 for each additional book

ALL PRICES INCLUDE U.S. POSTAGE/HANDLING

No. of books _____ x $_____ ea   = $_____
No. of books _____ x $_____ ea   = $_____
   Multi-book Discount   (%) $_____
SUBTOTAL $_____

☐ **Priority Mail (add $2.50 more for every 2 books)** $_____
   TOTAL ENCLOSED (check or money order) $_____

NAME_____ADDRESS_____

CITY_____STATE_____ZIP_____

Send check/Money Order to: Larsen's Outdoor Publishing,
Dept. BR99, 2640 Elizabeth Place, Lakeland, FL 33813
(Sorry, no credit card orders)

OUR COVER ARTIST: JOHN P. LEE

Many people say John Lee doesn't own a brush larger than a 000. He builds his paintings feather by feather, leaf by leaf, hair by hair...

A native of Chambers County, Alabama, John Lee lived the early years of his life next to nature on a farm where he became fascinated with the native wildlife. Spending many an hour hunting and fishing near his home, he drew and painted wildlife at an early age. Formal training in art began while Lee attended Samford University and then graduated from Troy State University with a Bachelor of Science degree in art education. Lee then taught art in the Hendry County, Florida, public schools for five years.

After working his way through college in law enforcement, Lee returned to a law enforcement career. Today he is chief of police at the University of Montevallo in Montevallo, Alabama. A master's degree in criminal justice administration, a graduate of the F.B.I. National Academy and over 20 years in law enforcement have provided the discipline necessary for Lee to render with such sharp detail the subject matter in his paintings. Through the use of small brush strokes, Lee constructs paintings in much the same manner as the Renaissance masters. Lee's work achieves a dimension and luminescence not commonly found today.

The winner of numerous art awards, John P. Lee can be reached at P.O. Box 92, Montevallo, Al 35115. Phone: 205- 665-2254.